Trees and Flowering Shrubs

of

Glacier National Park
and Surrounding Areas

**Also by Shannon Kimball
and Peter Lesica**

*Wildflowers of Glacier National Park
and Surrounding Areas*

Distributed by Mountain Press
Missoula, Montana
www.mountain-press.com

Trees and
Flowering Shrubs

of

Glacier National Park
and Surrounding Areas

Going-to-the-Sun Mountain

by
Shannon Kimball
and
Peter Lesica

© 2013 by Trillium Press, Kalispell, Montana.
Distributed by Mountain Press, Missoula, Montana.
Printed in China.

Cataloging-in-Publication data is on file at the Library of Congress.
ISBN 978-0-87842-604-1.

Back cover photographs of authors taken by John Kimball and Dave
Hanna. Photo of mountain pine beetle by Dave Hanna. Birch tree
infected with bronze birch borer taken by Shannon Kimball. All other
photographs, including front cover, taken by Peter Lesica.

DISCLAIMER: Consuming and/or using plants for medicinal pur-
poses is extremely dangerous and may result in death or serious injury.
The authors, publishers and distributors of this book do not recom-
mend experimentation with edible and medicinal plants by readers.

CONTENTS

DEDICATIONS

For Noah.
S.K.

To past and present natural resource managers at
Glacier National Park, including Jack Potter,
Carl Key, Laurie Kurth, Tara Carolin and Joyce Lapp.
P.L.

ACKNOWLEDGEMENTS

Thank you to many people who helped improve the quality of this book. Stephan Prince came up with the idea of a book that described all of the trees in Glacier National Park. Richard Menicke provided the map on the following page. Technical guidance was supplied by John Rimel and Jeannie Nuckolls of Mountain Press. Dave Hanna provided advice on photography. Amy Gannon shared her knowledge on tree diseases and insects. Anne Garde reviewed the manuscript.

Shannon appreciates the support of family and friends: John, Carolyn and Noah Kimball, Carol Stevens, Ralph Fitzpatrick, Quinn Anderson, Lisa McKeon, Mary Buenz, Wendy Anderson, Jen Asebrook, Jenny Tollefson and Kelly Davidson.

Waterton Lakes National Park

North
Fork

Kintla Lake

LIVINGSTON RANGE

Waterton Valley

Belly River

Blackfeet
Indian
Reservation

Bowman Lake

Quartz Lakes

Flathead

Polebridge

LEWIS

Lake
Sherburne

Many
Glacier

Logging Lake

River

Saint Mary

Inside North Fork Road

Rising
Sun

Camas Road

Camas Creek

Logan Pass

Flathead

Going-To-The-Sun Road

Saint Mary Lake

National

McGee
Meadow

Howe
Lake

Lake McDonald

Continental Divide

Cut Bank Creek

RANGE

Forest

West
Glacier

Nyack Creek

Two
Medicine

Middle

East
Glacier

Fork

Flathead

Marias Pass

River

Bob Marshall
Wilderness Complex

Glacier National Park

| 6 | 0 | 6 | 12 | 18 | Kilometers |

| 7 | 0 | 7 | 14 | Miles |

Introduction

Glacier National Park and the surrounding Northern Rocky Mountains are one of the most scenic and wild landscapes in North America. The Crown of the Continent, as this area is often called, still supports all of the native wildlife present when Europeans first arrived. Although the alpine areas, with their jagged peaks, knife-edge ridges, colorful rocks, and spectacular waterfalls, attract the most attention from visitors, it is the forests and shrublands that provide habitat for charismatic

wildlife such as grizzly bears, black bears, mountain lions, lynx, pine martins, and a host of eagles, hawks and songbirds. We hope that this book will help visitors to the area come to better know and understand the lives of the trees and shrubs that make up these important habitats.

Going-to-the-Sun Mountain

Glacier National Park was established in 1910 by an act of Congress. The park encompasses roughly 4,000 square kilometers (about a million acres). It is bordered by Canada's Waterton Lakes National Park to the north and the Bob Marshall Wilderness Complex, an extensive, protected wilderness area to the south. The mountains within Glacier National Park lie along the main range of the Rocky Mountains, with many peaks rising 8,000–10,000 feet (2,450–3,050 meters). The Continental Divide winds its way from northwest to southeast along the tallest peaks, separating the upper reaches of streams that flow into the Pacific and Atlantic oceans. A portion of a second divide, the Northern Divide, meanders through the eastern side of Glacier National Park, separating the Arctic and Atlantic oceans.

Climate and Geology

The high mountains of the Continental Divide act as a barrier separating two distinct weather patterns. The climate west of the Divide is most strongly influenced by a relatively warm and moist westerly flow from the Pacific Ocean. East of the Continental Divide, the climate is heavily influenced by drier, more inland weather systems and cold, arctic air masses pressing south from Canada. The resulting climate is markedly drier and colder on the east side of the Divide than on the west, although this difference is more apparent in the valleys and on the lower slopes than in the high mountains.

Most of the rock that underlies Glacier National Park and the surrounding mountains was formed from sediments deposited in what was once a shallow sea, 800 million to over a billion years ago in the Precambrian age. The deposits were folded and lifted 65–70 million years ago along an overthrust zone, creating a long band of solid rock running roughly northwest to southeast. The rugged mountains, steep slopes, narrow valleys and amphitheater-like cirque headwalls that characterize Glacier National Park were carved by the repeated advance and retreat of glaciers that covered the area during the last ice age. Today only about forty glaciers in the park continue to carve and reshape rock on a small scale. These glaciers are getting smaller, the result of a warming trend that is affecting most of our planet.

Mount Stimpson

Vegetation

Great variation in the Park's elevation combines with an extremely variable climate to create diverse habitats for a large number of plant communities. Many coniferous forests on the west side of the park have a warm coastal character, while forests on the east side are drier and more open. Valley bottomlands support riparian forests and thickets. Different species of woody plants occupy these varied habitats, providing insight into the role that climate and topography play in this fascinating landscape.

Elevation has a powerful impact on the development of vegetation. With increased elevation there is a decrease in temperature and an increase in wind and precipitation. These environmental factors are sometimes moderated in rugged, mountainous terrain. In Glacier National Park, elevation can be used to define three different vegetation zones. These zones and corresponding elevation ranges are:

Zone	Elevation Range
Montane	3,000-5,500 ft (915-1675 m)
Subalpine	5,000-7,500 ft (1525-2285 m)
Alpine	>6,500 ft (>1980 m)

The following is merely a summary of these three vegetation zones and the complex plant communities they support. A more detailed description of plant communities in all three zones is available in *A Flora of Glacier National Park* (Lesica 2002).

The **Montane Zone** in Glacier National Park and the surrounding area supports three distinct types of forests: riparian, aspen and coniferous. **Riparian forests** develop on the floodplains of rivers and large streams. They are dominated by black

Elizabeth Lake

cottonwood and many species of willow. New riparian forests are constantly regenerating as these waterways meander from one channel to another. **Aspen forests** are primarily found on the east side of Glacier National Park, near the eastern boundary. These deciduous woodlands often develop adjacent to grasslands and may cover extensive areas. Quaking aspen and black cottonwood are the dominant trees, but Engelmann spruce are sometimes present. **Coniferous forests** cover mountain slopes and benches and support many tree species, especially west of the Continental Divide. Lush forests dominated by western redcedar and western hemlock occur in the upper McDonald Valley. Moist forests of Douglas fir, western larch, and western white pine occur in warmer, somewhat drier sites. Ponderosa pine is found at the lowest elevations. Paper birch regenerates after fire and is also common in low-elevation forests west of the Divide. Serviceberry, oceanspray, thimbleberry and snowberry are common shrubs in these forests. Large areas along the North Fork of the Flathead River support dense stands of pure lodgepole pine continually regenerated by periodic wildfire. Coniferous forests east of the Divide at the lowest elevations are more typical of the subalpine zone. However, Douglas-fir forests occur in the vicinity of St. Mary. Wetlands, such as wet meadows, swamps, marshes and fens, occur within the forests and provide habitat for tall shrubs such as river birch, red osier dogwood, willows, gooseberries and alders.

Vast tracts of coniferous forest blanket mountain slopes throughout the **Subalpine Zone** of Glacier National Park. Most subalpine forests are dominated by subalpine fir, Engelmann spruce and lodgepole pine, but Douglas fir and western larch may also be common. Whitebark pine forests occupied higher subalpine sites prior to the last two decades, but disease has made these trees rare. Subalpine larch sometimes grows among subalpine fir. Huckleberry and fool's huckleberry are common understory shrubs. Higher subalpine forests subject to severe wind and snow accumulation often develop a stunted growth form called krummholz. Avalanche chutes filled with tall, flexible shrubs such as mountain ash, alder, elderberry and Rocky Mountain maple are common in steep ravines where snow slides downhill in the spring. Avalanche chutes are visible on high mountain slopes along Going-to-the Sun Road.

The harsh climate of the **Alpine Zone** severely limits plant growth, especially for woody plants. Dwarf subalpine fir or Engelmann spruce trees are sometimes found in sheltered sites. The only common woody plants are small-statured or dwarf shrubs such as arctic willow, rock willow, mountain avens and kinnikinnick.

Disturbances

Wildfire has a tremendous impact on the structure and composition of forested areas throughout Glacier National Park in all vegetation zones. Burned montane and subalpine forests of Engelmann spruce and subalpine fir give way to monocultures of lodgepole pine, a tree that establishes abundantly after severe fire. Given enough time, these forests may return to spruce and fir as the lodgepole ages and succumbs to insects and disease, or frequent fire may maintain the lodgepole dominance. Most understory plants will survive fire, but the immediate post-fire appearance of the understory changes dramatically. Herbaceous species like fireweed and showy aster recover quickly and bloom prolifically in the full sun. Gradually the resident shrubs resprout, and the trees regain dominance. Older Douglas fir, western larch and ponderosa pine have thick, fire-resistant bark and may survive low- to moderate-intensity wildfire, resulting in multiple-age stands after several bouts of wildfire. In some situations, open, park-like stands of mature fire-resistant trees can develop.

Forests can also be severely affected by boring or leaf-eating **insects**. Mountain pine beetle outbreaks have occurred sporadically in Glacier National Park and the surrounding area. In the past these insects have damaged mainly ponderosa pine and lodgepole pine at lower elevations. Warmer weather of recent years has allowed mountain pine beetles to attack higher-elevation lodgepole and whitebark pine stands. Spruce budworm defoliates the branch tips of Engelmann spruce and Douglas fir, doing more damage to the latter. Historically these insects have done little permanent damage to forests, but recent outbreaks have severely damaged or even killed Douglas fir. Other insects, such as spruce adelgid and bronze birch borer, have less dramatic effects on Glacier's forests.

Diseases of trees caused by native fungi, bacteria or viruses, such as rusts, cankers, root rots or heart rots are common but usually only have a significant impact on old or overcrowded trees. The same cannot be said for the non-native white pine blister rust. This fungus attacks all five-needle pines and has killed nearly all of the western white pine and whitebark pine in Glacier National Park and much of the northern Rocky Mountains. Most of the large dead trees in upper subalpine forests are whitebark pine killed by blister rust.

Six pests and diseases that are particularly affecting trees in and around Glacier National Park are White Pine Blister Rust, Mountain Pine Beetle, Western Spruce Budworm, Dwarf Mistletoe, Cooley Spruce Gall Adelgid and Bronze Birch Borer. Each of these diseases/pests are further discussed in the following section.

How to Use This Book

Trees and shrubs are separated into different sections; trees appear first. The tree section begins with needle-leaved species. Broad-leaved trees follow. Every tree in Glacier National Park appears in this book.

Shrubs are separated by flower color. The different color groups are represented by colored tabs at the tops of pages. Cone-bearing shrubs, such as common juniper, are included with the brown- and green-colored flowering species. Catkin-producing shrubs, like birch and willow, are also placed in the brown and green section, following the cone-bearers.

Since willows are difficult to distinguish, an "Introduction to Willows" appears immediately before the willow species. This section describes specific willow characteristics that will help in their identification.

Guidelines and Safety Precautions

While this book makes reference to edible and medicinal qualities of plants, **the authors strongly discourage collecting and using any part of a plant as food or medicine.** Picking flowers in Glacier National Park is not permitted. A small quantity of berries may be gathered, but save larger harvests for public land outside the Park. Check with Park staff for the most current berry-collection rules.

White Pine Blister Rust

White pine blister rust has been described by some forest pathologists as the most destructive disease of five-needle pines in North America. It is caused by the infection of a fungus, *Cronartium ribicola*. In Glacier National Park the disease has primarily impacted whitebark pine and limber pine. Western white pine has also been affected in the Park and in surrounding forests of Montana and northern Idaho. In other regions of the United States and Canada blister rust has devastated eastern white pine, sugar pine and southwestern white pine populations.

Whitebark Pine Infected with Blister Rust

Scientists believe blister rust is native to Asia. By the late 19th century the fungus had found its way to European forests, where it began killing trees. Scientists estimate that blister rust was introduced to North America around 1900, when infected nursery stock from France entered a port near Vancouver, Canada. By the 1950s it had spread to five-needle pines throughout the western United States, where it was severely impacting forest health.

The fungus that causes blister rust disease in trees has an interesting and very complex life cycle, involving five spore stages and two host plants. The first plant host is a pine tree (*Pinus* spp.); the second plant host is not so straightforward. For decades researchers thought that the second plant host was currant (*Ribes* spp.). However, recent evidence suggests that other plants, such as paintbrush (*Castilleja* spp.), may be able to act as secondary hosts for the fungus, as well. While persistent infection is lethal for pines, the fungus does not appear to negatively affect currant or paintbrush.

In late summer or early fall a basidiospore infects a tree by coming into contact with one of its needles. The basidiospore enters the needle surface through a small pore, then moves into the branch or trunk. Here it produces a dense network of filamentous strands (hyphae), forming a swollen canker. Spermatia (a second, different type of spore) are produced at the edges of the canker in late summer or early fall. The following spring aeciospores (a third, different type of spore) are produced at the edges of the canker. The bark around the canker dies and the fungus moves into adjacent, live bark. Additional spermatia and aeciospores form on this tree in late summer and spring, as years pass. Eventually the branch or entire tree is girdled and dies.

Whitebark Pine Branch Infected with Blister Rust

The bright yellow aeciospores can travel hundreds of miles on the wind, but they can't infect pines. The only species known to become infected by these particular spores are species of currant (also known as gooseberry) and possibly paintbrush. These species are common in white pine forests. Aeciospores infect the secondary host's leaves in the spring, sometimes producing yellowish spots. The infection is usually inconspicuous. Two more spore types (urediniospores and teliospores) are produced on the secondary host as the summer progresses. Neither of these spores can infect pines. In the fall, however, production of basidiospores occurs. These spores disperse in the wind and start the cycle over again by infecting pine trees.

A widespread program to eliminate currant was undertaken from 1916 to 1967, in an attempt to control the spread of blister rust disease to native pines. The program was costly and employed thousands of field workers digging up currants on mountain slopes across the west, but was never successful.

More recent management of blister rust infection has focused on disease prevention through genetic selection. This technique involves identifying trees that have remained healthy in an area of rampant disease, and may have a higher degree of genetic resistance to the fungus. Cones are harvested from these trees, the seeds extracted and planted, and the seedlings grown in a well-controlled environment. The seedlings are then planted back into their original forested habitats. Forest managers hope that these trees, having higher natural resistance to blister rust disease, will establish and produce disease-resistant offspring. Glacier National Park initiated such a program in 1997, with the intention of rehabilitating its limber and whitebark pine populations. Seeds from both pine species were harvested, propagated in a plant nursery, and planted in appropriate habitats as seedlings. In some areas seeds were directly planted.

The Park has an extensive monitoring program in place to evaluate the results of this project. To date, limber pine restoration using these methods has been disappointing, with very low survival rates of transplanted seedlings. The seedlings appear to have succumbed to the harsh conditions into which they were planted, perhaps unable to withstand the transition from life in a plant nursery to the Park's severe environment.

Whitebark pine seedlings have fared relatively well, compared to limber pine, with much higher survival rates. Park researchers Jen Asebrook and Jen Hintz believe that the environmental conditions into which the whitebark pine seedlings were planted are not as harsh and exposed as those of limber pine, giving the whitebark seedlings a better chance to establish at the new sites. Germination and establishment of seeds planted directly in the ground has not yet occurred in revegetation sites. Monitoring is in place to evaluate this planting technique, as well.

Mountain Pine Beetle

In recent years our forests have experienced widespread outbreaks of mountain pine beetle (*Dendroctonus ponderosae*). This insect has affected many forests across the northwest US and western Canada, notably changing the appearance of our forested landscapes. Many stands have been completely decimated by this beetle, leaving hundreds of acres of standing dead trees.

Mature lodgepole pine trees are most often the target of mountain pine beetle. But the beetles also attack other pine species, such as ponderosa, limber and whitebark pines. Pine beetles have had dramatic effects on these and other species in some parts of Montana and adjacent Canada, but the dramatic outbreaks we see, where millions of trees are killed across mountain slopes, are generally areas forested with lodgepole pine.

Beetle-killed Lodgepole Pine

The range of mountain pine beetle destruction stretches from the Canadian forests of British Columbia and Alberta, south to forested regions of Arizona and New Mexico. It is primarily a western epidemic, though it has the potential to spread into pines of eastern North America, such as jack pine (*Pinus banksiana*).

Native to western North America, a mountain pine beetle is about 5 mm long and has a hard, black exoskeleton. Its size is often described as being comparable to a grain of rice. A beetle spends only a few days in the outside world. The majority of the insect's life is spent burrowed under tree bark, moving through four different growth forms as it progress through its life cycle.

In mid-summer female beetles bore through the bark and into the sapwood of healthy, mature trees. As a female bores into an individual tree, she releases a pheromone (chemical) signal that is sensed by nearby male and female mountain pine beetles, attracting them to the tree. These beetles join in the tree attack, releasing more pheromones, and at-tracting more beetles. The beetles release a different pheromone once a tree is "full," ensuring the tree won't be overcrowded, and their larvae will have sufficient food.

"Flushing" of a Mountain Pine Beetle
(photo courtesy of Dave Hanna)

Female beetles construct galleries (interconnected tunnels) in the phloem of the tree, between the bark and the sapwood. Here a female mates with a male beetle, then deposits pearly-white eggs. The eggs hatch into worm-like larvae that feed on the phloem of the tree. Since tree phloem is such a poor nutrition source, the larvae's diet is supple-mented with a fungus, commonly called the blue-stain fungus. Fungal fragments are brought in by the adult beetles, tucked into their exo-skeleton. When the female tunnels into the tree bark to lay her eggs, she also deposits these fungal fragments. Blue-stain fungus colonizes the phloem and sapwood of the infected tree, converting the tree's sap into nutritious food for the beetle larvae.

The legless larvae create more galleries in the phloem as they feed through the winter and spring months. When they mature, in early summer, they form oval-shaped cells in the phloem. Within these cells the larvae turn into pupae, then into adult beetles which continue to feed within the phloem for several days. Adult beetles emerge from the tree by tunneling out of the bark.

The initial response of a tree to a mountain pine beetle attack is to "flush" the beetles out with sap. Clumps of dried pitch are often observed near holes where pine beetles have bored into the bark of a tree.

A healthy tree can entrap numerous marauders in sap, but if beetles are abundant they will eventually be able to overcome the tree's resources. Once the beetle has entered the tree, created galleries and laid her eggs, the tree phloem is dramatically impaired. Because the phloem is responsible for transporting water from tree roots to the leaves and branches, its destruction spells disaster for the tree. The blue-stain fungus also damages and clogs the phloem as it colonizes and digests these cells.

Climate change and fire suppression have made pine trees more vulnerable to beetle attacks. A healthy tree may be able to ward off an attack, but a tree stressed by drought, overcrowding and old age usually succumbs to an all-out pine beetle assault. Many western forests have recently experienced prolonged drought, which has weakened tree defenses. Fire suppression, a common forest management practice since the early 20th century, has resulted in vast tracts of mature lodgepole pine that are very susceptible to pine beetle outbreaks because the trees are crowded too closely together and nearing the end of their natural lifespan.

Beetle-killed Lodgepole Pine in Northwest Montana

A warming climate may be bad for pines, but it is good for beetles. Since forests are experiencing climate-induced stress, including frequent drought conditions, mountain pine beetle outbreaks are becoming more prevalent. Early-fall freezes and sustained cold temperatures are the natural regulatory mechanism that previously controlled epidemic outbreaks. These conditions have been all but absent since the mid-1980s, creating an environment where pine beetle populations can flourish. Scientists estimate that the current outbreak is ten times worse than previously recorded pine beetle outbreaks.

Many forest managers consider mountain pine beetle to be the most aggressive and destructive insect in the western US and Canada. In order to minimize damage to live trees, managers have developed prescriptions for treatment of diseased stands and prevention of further infestation. Methods typically involve removal of diseased trees before the wood becomes unmarketable and the beetles spread to other healthy trees. The application of chemical pesticides and pheromones that fend off beetles has also been used, but with limited success.

Mountain pine beetle outbreaks are also controlled by the amount of available food. With so much mature lodgepole pine available to beetles their population size has grown. Once this food source has been eliminated their numbers will likely decline.

Western Spruce Budworm

Widespread outbreaks of western spruce budworm (*Choristoneura occidentalis*) have resulted in extensive tree defoliation across western North America. United States Forest Service entomologists describe western spruce budworm as the "most widely distributed and destructive defoliator of coniferous forests in western North America." It impacts forests of the Rocky Mountains from Canada to Arizona and New Mexico, as well as in Washington and Oregon.

Spruce budworm is native to North America, and has historically been a natural part of the forested landscape. The insects primarily affect Douglas fir and grand fir. They impact subalpine fir, spruce and larch to a lesser extent, and serious outbreaks sometimes affect native pine species, such as ponderosa and western white pine.

The lifecycle of a spruce budworm begins in the fall when an adult moth, mottled brown in color and about an inch long, lays clusters of 25 to 40 eggs on the underside of tree needles. The eggs hatch into larvae after about ten days. The tiny larvae crawl into crevasses under bark scales and lichen, spin silky shelters (called hibernaculae), and slumber through the winter.

Spruce Budworm Defoliation of Tree Top

Tiny larvae emerge in early spring and crawl to branch tips where they begin to satisfy their voracious appetites by feeding on buds. They prefer soft, new needle growth, often entering developing buds before new needles have emerged. As new needles elongate the budworm larvae continue to feed. They often spin webs around clusters of foliage, creating a protective pocket within which they devour foliage.

As early summer days pass by, the larvae continue to feed and grow. In the later larval stage they are about 1 inch long and brown, with a pair of white spots on each body segment. In early to mid July (depending on elevation) they pupate, emerging as adult moths in late July to early August. Moths do not feed on trees; they mate then lay eggs in late fall, starting the cycle all over again. Male moths die after mating; females after laying eggs. The insect's full life cycle is completed in approximately 12 months.

Tree defoliation starts from the top and outer branch tips and works its way toward the trunk as the larvae work their way along branches. Mature trees can withstand up to 75% defoliation without dying, though the stress of defoliation reduces their ability to photosynthesize and makes them vulnerable to diseases and other insects. Younger trees are much more vulnerable to death by defoliation.

Douglas Fir Impacted by
Spruce Budworm

Periodic outbreaks of spruce budworm are natural. But the duration and severity of recent outbreaks, in which many trees are actually killed, have been higher than in past decades. Scientists speculate that fire suppression, which has dramatically altered forest structure, has significantly contributed to outbreaks in recent years.

Before fire suppression was initiated, the understory of forests was much more open, as younger trees were periodically removed by low-intensity fire. Fire suppression has resulted in the formation of "layered" forests, where shade-tolerant species like Douglas fir and grand fir form multi-aged stands of mature trees, saplings and seedlings. Spruce budworms thrive under these conditions, dropping from mature trees to lower, young trees, devouring their tender leaves.

The mechanisms for regulating naturally occurring outbreaks include cold and wet weather conditions, predators and insect parasites. However, these mechanisms are overridden when climatic conditions and forest structure are optimal for increases in budworm population. Thinning saplings in stands of Douglas fir and grand fir has been explored as a preventative measure, as well as removing trees that are more susceptible to budworm (Douglas fir and grand fir) and leaving less susceptible trees (western larch and various pine species). Short term results of these manipulations have been mixed; the long-term results are not yet known.

Dwarf Mistletoe

Dwarf mistletoes (*Arceuthobium* spp.) are native, leafless, parasitic plants that grow on several different tree species in forests of the Northern Rocky Mountains. Tree species that often play host to mistletoes include ponderosa pine, lodgepole pine, limber pine, Douglas fir and western larch. In and around Glacier National Park species of mistletoe have had their largest impact on ponderosa pine, lodgepole pine and Douglas fir.

Each species of dwarf mistletoe is relatively host-specific, preferring one species of tree as its primary host. For example, Douglas fir is the primary tree infected by Douglas fir dwarf mistletoe (*Arceuthobium douglasii*). The ranges of dwarf mistletoes follow the ranges of trees that they infect, from the Rocky Mountain forests of British Columbia and Alberta southward to Colorado. Mistletoes are also found in the Cascade Range of Washington and Oregon, and the Sierra Range of Northern California.

Dwarf Mistletoe Plant on Whitebark Pine

Dwarf mistletoe infects a host tree by sending roots under tree bark, enabling the mistletoe plant to absorb water and nutrients from the tree's transport system: its xylem and phloem. The initial infection may produce a slight swelling of the bark at the infection site. Two to three years later mistletoe shoots appear, 0.5 to 6 inches long and less than 0.25 inch in diameter. The shoots range in color from olive or yellowish green to reddish brown.

A single mistletoe plant produces either male or female flowers (mon-oecious), but not both (dioecious). When the shoots flower, typically in the spring, they are pollinated by insects and wind. Female flowers produce berry-like fruit which contain a single seed. As it matures hy-drostatic pressure builds inside the fruit. In late August to mid-September the elastic outer case of the fruit bursts, propelling the seed into the air at high speed (up to 60 miles per hour). Seeds can travel up to 30 feet, but typically fall within 10 to 15 feet of the parent plant.

"Witches' Broom" on Douglas Fir

Seeds are coated with a sticky substance that helps them adhere to the surfaces on which they land. Some seeds are lost to the forest floor, but some land on the needles of neighboring trees. Rain washes away the sticky coating and allows the seed to slide down to the twig. In the spring these seeds germinate, sending roots into the twig bark to produce another dwarf mistletoe plant. Seeds may also be transported on the feathers of birds and fur of small mammals.

Dense areas of tree branch growth, called "witches' brooms," indicate a severe dwarf mistletoe infection. As the mistletoe roots extract nutri-ents from uninfected parts of the tree, vigor is reduced and tree growth slows. The crown dies as witches' brooms on lower branches extract more nutrients and water. Insects, such as mountain pine beetle, often attack trees heavily infected by mistletoe. The end result is almost always tree death.

Dwarf mistletoes also harm overall forest health by reducing seed production in host trees. Commercial wood production, in forests outside national parks, is adversely affected because the invading root system causes commercially unacceptable deformities and poor wood quality.

Branch pruning and tree removal are the most common methods of managing dwarf mistletoe infection. Pruning the lowest and largest witches' brooms from trees that are only moderately infected can add decades to the life of these trees. Tree removal is necessary in larger trees, where infected branches can't be reached, and in cases where infection is very severe. Special disposal of pruning debris is not necessary; mistletoe shoots die as soon as the tree branches are cut.

Douglas Fir Killed by Dwarf Mistletoe

Cooley Spruce Gall Adelgid

Cooley spruce gall adelgids are tiny insects closely related to aphids. Native to North America, adelgids spend most of their lives on spruce and Douglas fir trees, and occur wherever these two species grow. In northwest Montana adelgids damage Engelmann spruce and ornamental spruces, producing galls that resemble small cones at the ends of branches. They also affect Douglas fir, but the damage isn't as apparent.

The adelgid life cycle is complex, taking two years to complete and requiring both spruce and Douglas fir as host trees. These trees support five different life forms of the insect; three occur on spruce and two on Douglas fir.

On spruce trees, immature female adelgids spend the winter at the bases of terminal buds. They mature in early spring and lay hundreds of eggs near the tips of twigs. In about ten days the eggs hatch into hungry nymphs which migrate to the base of newly produced needles and start to devour the tender tissue. The twigs swell in response to

the feeding nymphs, pro- ducing a pine- apple shaped structure that encloses the nymphs. The nymphs feed on sap flowing to the damaged twig, while enjoying full protection from insect preda- tors, sheltered inside the gall. Here they ma- ture through the early months

Cooley Spruce Adelgid Infection in Engelmann Spruce Twig

of summer. By mid-summer the gall is brown and about an inch and a half long. Mature nymphs escape through small holes in the gall at the base of needles. They then molt into winged adelgids, and fly to Douglas fir or other spruce trees.

On Douglas fir trees female adelgids lay eggs on the needles. The eggs hatch and insects mature into both winged and wingless forms that feed on sap and soft tissue at the base of the Douglas fir needles. A gall is not formed on Douglas fir twigs. Instead, the adelgid produc- es a white, wooly cover that protects it as it feeds. These wooly spots can often be observed on infested needles.

In late summer winged adelgids fly back to spruce trees, where they lay eggs that hatch into an overwintering population. Wingless forms remain on Douglas fir. Here they lay eggs that hatch into a population that remains on Douglas fir over the winter.

The brown, deformed spruce branch tips, which look remarkably like cones, persist on the tree. Cooley spruce gall adelgids rarely kill a tree, but severe infestations slow tree growth and affect the appearance of spruce trees used for landscaping. Trees that are experiencing stress due to drought may be more at risk of a severe adelgid attack.

Several methods have been developed to control the Cooley spruce gall adelgid, primarily for use in the commercial horticulture trade. Trees that appear to be resistant to adelgid infection are often chosen for increased reproduction. The pruning of galls before they turn brown is also useful, especially in trees with a small number of galls. Insecticide sprays have also proven beneficial when applied in the fall and early spring.

Bronze Birch Borer

Paper birch trees (*Betula papyrifera*, pg. 62) with dead and dying branches at the top are a common sight along streams and in moist forests in and around Glacier National Park. These trees are most likely being attacked by insects called bronze birch borers. Though their most obvious damage is inflicted upon our native paper birch trees, birch borers will attack any native or non-native species of birch, including ornamental birch trees.

The bronze birch borer (*Agrilus anxius*) is native to North America. Adult beetles are almost ½ inch long, olive-brown in color, and have bronze iridescence. Male beetles are smaller than females and have a greenish head. The heads of female beetles are coppery brown. They are common in southern Canada, and across the northern United States, wherever birches grow.

Female beetles lay eggs in the cracks of birch bark during the summer. Larvae hatch about 2 weeks later and begin to excavate a tunnel into the phloem and cambium of the tree. The larvae are slender, worm-like, pearly white and grow to about 1½ inches at maturity. As they feed they make meandering tunnels (galleries) in the inner tree bark. In the fall they stop feeding and overwinter in the galleries, then resume feeding in early spring. Mature larvae pupate in the xylem of the tree in May and June. Pupa start out creamy white, then darken as they mature into adult beetles. Adult beetles emerge from late June to mid-July, through D-shaped holes in the bark. The entire life cycle takes 1 or 2 years, depending on geographic location, temperature and the health of the host tree. Two years are usually required in areas where the growing season is short and climate is cool, and in vigorous, healthy host trees.

Tree damage occurs when beetle larvae feed on the inner bark of the tree. The production of extensive galleries in the phloem disrupts the transport of sugars and other

Paper Birch Infected by Bronze Birch Borer

metabolic products from the leaves to the roots. Eventually part of the root system dies. Branches at the tree top die because a damaged root system can't supply them with adequate water. A tree that is unable to withstand a birch borer attack often dies within several years.

Trees under stress are more vulnerable to mortality from bronze birch borer infestation. The defenses of adult trees may be weakened by drought, soil compaction, or a stem or root injury. The root systems of birches are particularly susceptible to drought and physical damage of birches are particularly susceptible to drought and physical damage because they are very shallow. Paper birch trees are generally short-lived, so older trees are often less healthy and vulnerable to a birch borer attack.

Defoliation by other insects can also weaken tree defenses. Healthy trees may be able to withstand a birch borer attack by producing dense callus tissue around the larvae feeding gallery. The callus prevents the larvae from expanding the feeding gallery and eventually kills them by eliminating their food supply.

Land managers in national parks and forests are encouraged to practice prevention when managing the relationship between birch trees and the bronze birch borer. The maintenance of healthy birch trees requires leaving them alone and giving them some space, since they are very sensitive to disturbance. Mechanical thinning around birch trees is generally discouraged due to the risk of damage to the tree's shallow root system. In cases where birch borers have already set in, the removal of heavily infested trees and/or trimming of dead and dying branches is recommended in the spring, before adult beetles emerge. This practice is thought to reduce the level of infestation in a localized area.

Rocky Mountain Juniper
Juniperus scopulorum
Cedar Family (Cupressaceae)

Growth Form: Our only tree-like juniper, Rocky Mountain juniper exhibits great variation in crown shape. It is typically conical or elongate growing as a single-stemmed tree, though it sometimes has a gnarled, bushy appearance. It may also grow with multiple stems sprouting from the trunk base, giving the crown a highly irregular appearance. Mature trees range in height from 15–20 feet. It is often referred to as a tall shrub.

Bark: Reddish brown, thin and stringy. Long, thin pieces peel away from stem.

Cones: Male and female cones are produced on separate trees. Female cones are fleshy, bluish green and berry-like with a waxy outer coating. They are about ¼ inch long and often referred to as "juniper berries." Inconspicuous, pollen-bearing male cones are produced at branch tips.

Bark

Leaves: Seedlings and immature plants produce sharply pointed, awl-like leaves about ½ inch long. They are not jointed where the leaf meets the stem, in contrast to a similar species, common juniper (a low-growing shrub, pg. 78). Older trees have compressed, scale-like leaves that grow in pairs along twigs. The foliage is green to yellowish green and often thinly covered by a whitish, waxy compound. Leaves are strongly aromatic when crushed.

Leaves and Berries

Habitat and Range: Rocky Mountain juniper prefers open sites and is intolerant of shade. It occurs in dry, open woodlands and in stony soil along streams at lower elevations. It often grows with ponderosa pine (*Pinus ponderosa*, pg. 52). Rocky Mountain juniper grows from southwestern Alberta and central British Columbia, south through Montana and Idaho, to New Mexico.

Pests and Disease: Cedar-apple rust is a fungal disease that is common in junipers, including this species. The fungus requires two hosts to complete its life cycle, spending part of its life cycle on a juniper host and part on a host in the rose family.

Cedar-apple Rust

Rocky Mountain Juniper

Notes: Rocky Mountain juniper berries are the primary winter food of Townsend's solitaire. The berries are a popular winter/spring food source for many other birds, including robins, evening grosbeaks, wild turkeys and grouse. Seeds only germinate after they have passed through the digestive tract of a bird or another animal. The wood is resistant to rot. Small-diameter stems were used extensively for fence posts before the advent of inexpensive metal posts. This tree's thin bark makes it highly susceptible to fire. Trees are extremely slow-growing and can tolerate harsh, drought conditions. A Rocky Mountain juniper near Logan, Utah is estimated to be 3,000 years old. It is 36 feet tall and 6½ feet in diameter. Look for this species on dry, older terraces along the North and Middle Forks of the Flathead River, and on rocky slopes in the McDonald Valley.

Western Red Cedar
Thuja plicata
Cedar Family (Cupressaceae)

Growth Form: Mature trees have a conical crown and a trunk that is often swollen and buttressed at the base. Height of mature western red cedar is 100–150 feet. The root system is shallow and extensive. The crown is broadly conical when growing in open areas, but narrowly conical in more closed stands of trees.

Bark: Thin and peeling from the tree in strips. Young trees have reddish-brown bark. Bark of mature trees is gray.

Bark

Cones: Male and female cones are produced on the same tree. Female cones are less than a half inch long, egg-shaped and have 4 to 6 pairs of spine-tipped scales that spread apart to release the seeds. Seeds have 2 lateral wings. Male cones are reddish and tiny (less than ¼ inch long). They are produced at branch tips.

Leaves: Sprays of flattened, glossy-green foliage cascade from spreading branches. Individual leaves are scale-like and overlap each other in pairs along each twig. The foliage is strongly aromatic, especially when crushed, making it a favorite for Christmas wreaths and garlands.

Leaves and Cones

Habitat and Range: Western red cedar trees require high soil moisture to survive and are very tolerant of shady conditions. In Glacier National Park and the northern Rocky Mountains they occur in moist forests and along shady streams. In areas with high precipitation, such as north Idaho and adjacent Montana and British Columbia, western red cedar occurs on cool slopes. Its range extends from Alberta and British Columbia through Idaho and Montana. It also grows in the Coast and Cascade Ranges from southeastern Alaska to northern California.

Pests and Disease: Western red cedar has relatively few significant pathogens. Bark beetles will inhabit cedar trees, but infestations are typically low-grade and rarely fatal. Trees that are stressed due to drought conditions or root compaction may be more susceptible to bark beetle infestations. Although western redcedar has chemical resistance to fungi, old trees may still be attacked by rot at their base. Hollow trunk bases may then be occupied by wood ants. Large holes can often be seen at the base of cedar trees where pileated woodpeckers have searched for these insects.

Western Red Cedar

Notes: In the northern Rockies western red cedar is limited to the moistest sites with little disturbance, like the McDonald Valley in Glacier National Park. It is much more prevalent in forests of the Pacific Northwest and northern Idaho. Because anti-fungal compounds in the tree make it very resistant to rot, its wood is used extensively for shingles and other weather-exposed building applications. As a result, old-growth cedar trees are uncommon, except in protected areas such as national parks and wilderness areas. Native Americans used this tree extensively. Tree trunks were carved for totem poles and dugout canoes. Teas made from the boughs have been used to treat cold symptoms and diarrhea.

Grand Fir
Abies grandis
Pine Family (Pinaceae)

Growth Form: Mature grand fir trees have a broadly conical crown, and grow to about 160 feet. They produce branches in flattened sprays. Seedlings and saplings are much more common than large trees, because the trees are susceptible to disease and don't live very long.

Bark: Young trees have smooth, light gray bark dotted with resin blisters. As trees mature the bark splits, forming a pattern of long, slender, vertical segments across the trunk.

Cones: Green seed cones are cylindrical and 2–4 inches long. In mid- to late-autumn the cones turn brown. Mature cones are rarely available for examination because they are produced at the tops of tall, old trees and disintegrate in place.

Bark

Needles: Foliage is soft to the touch. Flattened sprays form on lower branches because needles grow from the sides of twigs. On upper branches the needles curve upward. Individual needles are flattened and blunt. Needles are ¾– 2 inches long. The upper surface is dark and shiny green. The lower surface is lighter green and has two whitish stripes of stomata that run the length of the leaf.

Needles

Habitat and Range: Grand fir is very shade tolerant, so it grows well in the understory of forests dominated by other trees. In the Park it occupies low- to mid-elevation, moist forests. Grand fir is more common in the Swan and Flathead Valleys, south of the Park. Thickets of saplings often form under the canopy of forests where fire has been excluded. Its range includes the Coastal and Cascade Ranges of the Pacific Northwest. It also grows in the northern Rocky Mountains, where its range extends from southeastern British Columbia to Idaho and Wyoming.

Pests and Disease: Grand fir succumbs to a variety of insect and fungal pathogens. Fir engraver beetles enter the bark at the base of a tree then lay horizontal egg galleries in the sapwood. Once the eggs hatch, beetle larvae form vertical galleries, further damaging the flow of water and nutrients. The balsam woolly adelgid attacks the bark of grand fir, producing a growth-stimulating reaction as the tree attempts to rid itself of the insect. Growth of heart rot into the sapwood occurs, inhibiting water and nutrient flow throughout the entire tree. Dense growth in tree branches, called witches broom, is produced by a fungal "rust" pathogen.

Grand Fir

Notes: Without fire and disease grand fir would mature into the dominant tree species in many moist, low-elevation sites. It rarely attains dominance because sun-tolerant species that establish after fire, such as Douglas fir and western larch, are much more resistant to disease and fire. Grand fir isn't widely used in construction because the wood is soft compared to other tree species. However it does produce fine pulp, which is used in high-quality paper. Its soft wood makes it an ideal home for cavity-dwelling birds, such as pileated woodpeckers. Grand fir hybridizes with white fir (*A. concolor* var. *lowiana* or *A. lowiana*) in forests west of the northern Rockies, on sites where both trees are common.

Subalpine Fir
Abies lasiocarpa
Pine Family (Pinaceae)

Growth Form: Subalpine fir has a slender, spire-like growth form that enables the tree to shed snow as it accumulates on upper boughs. It grows up to 130 feet and is the dominant tree in high-elevation forests and narrow canyons where cool air settles. At treeline it also dominates the vegetation, forming "krummholz" stands of short, shrubby trees. Patches of wind-scoured trees often form thickets around high-elevation meadows and rock outcrops. Branches that are held down by snow often take root and send up shoots, forming new, stubby trees.

Bark: Light gray and smooth with scattered resin blisters. Older trees have shallow, vertical cracks.

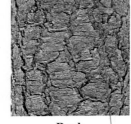
Bark

Cones: Dark purple cones develop in late summer and sit erect on upper branch tips. They are cylindrical and 2½–4 inch long. Sticky pitch often covers the cones, giving them a shiny, "glazed" appearance. The cones disintegrate on the tree, so will be observed on the ground only if they have been cut and dropped by red squirrels.

Needles: Its dark green needles are about 1 inch long. They grow from all sides of the twig, but are twisted upward toward the top of the branch. Both sides of the needles bear visible lines of white stomata, which enable the tree to absorb carbon dioxide and release oxygen, and to give off water vapor through transpiration. The foliage is relatively soft to the touch.

Needles and Cones

Habitat and Range: Subalpine fir is abundant in the Park's subalpine forests, where it grows as a spire-shaped tree. It is also common in krummholz shrublands of the alpine zone. It grows extensively at high altitude in the Rocky Mountains of British Columbia and Alberta. Its range extends south into the mountains of the Pacific Northwest and Intermountain West.

Snow Mold

Pests and Disease: Dark mats of "snow mold" are often seen covering portions of subalpine fir trees as the snow recedes. These mats are produced by cold-tolerant fungi that flourish in the moist, sheltered environment created by snow-laden tree boughs. The fungal communities are ephemeral and disappear once the snow is completely melted. Tree damage includes death of foliage and branches covered by snow mold. The fungus sometimes kills seedlings and saplings.

Subalpine Fir

Notes: Subalpine fir and Douglas fir (pg. 54) can be distinguished from each other by looking at the buds (at branch tips) and cones. The buds of subalpine fir are blunt, while those of Douglas fir are sharp-pointed. Cones of subalpine fir sit erect on branches, while Douglas fir cones hang from branches. Subalpine fir cones lack the 3-pronged bracts that protrude from the scales of Douglas fir cones. The Blackfeet Indians used the resin produced by subalpine fir to treat fevers and colds and as incense. Other tribes pounded the needles and mixed them with deer fat, forming a salve that was used on open wounds. The bark of subalpine fir is thin, making it very susceptible to mortality by wildfire.

Subalpine Larch
Larix lyallii
Pine Family (Pinaceae)

Growth Form: Mature subalpine larch trees are short compared to other conifers, growing only up to 65 feet tall. They have straight, slender trunks. Branching is irregular, likely caused by exposure to high winds. Like western larch (*L. occidentalis*, pg. 40) the foliage of subalpine larch turns golden yellow in late fall, and is shed in early winter.

Bark: Bark of mature trees is covered with purplish to reddish brown, flaky scales. The bark of subalpine larch isn't as thick as that of the more fire-resistant western larch. It is usually only about 1 inch at its thickest point, near the tree base.

Bark

Cones: Seed cones vary in color from yellowish brown to purplish red. They are 1½– 2 inches long, and bear long, slender bracts protruding beyond the cone scales.

Needles: Soft, bright green needles are bundled together into tufts, with 30-40 needles per bundle. Tufts protrude from the ends of stubby twigs that grow along branches. Needles have 4 sides in cross-section.

Needles and Cones

Habitat and Range: Stands of subalpine larch occur at or near treeline. Uniform stands often grow in shallow glades where snow lies until late in the spring. In Glacier National Park, stands of subalpine larch occupy areas around Boulder Pass and Goat Haunt. In Canada it primarily occurs along the Continental Divide in British Columbia and Alberta. In the United States, subalpine larch grows in high-elevation forests of the Cascades in northern Washington, and in the Rocky Mountains of western Montana and central Idaho.

Pests and Disease: Subalpine larch is relatively free of significant, terminal disease and pests. Violent winds often damage crowns in conjunction with clinging ice and snow. The larch casebearer, which defoliates western larch does not significantly threaten subalpine larch. Casebearer beetle larvae, which feed on leaf tissue, cannot tolerate the extremely low temperatures common in the high-elevation habitat of subalpine larch. Larch needle cast, a fungus that develops on larch needles, can discolor needles and reduce growth rate in infected trees.

Subalpine Larch

Notes: Habitat is the most obvious way to differentiate subalpine larch from western larch. Subalpine larch is clearly a tree of higher elevation. The cones of subalpine larch are typically longer than those of western larch. Perhaps the best way to distinguish the two species is to examine the youngest twigs. New twigs of subalpine larch are densely covered with long, tangled hair, appearing almost wooly. The new twigs of western larch are hairless or lightly covered with shorter hair. Subalpine larch is sometimes called alpine larch. Blue grouse are reported to feed heavily on subalpine larch needles.

Western Larch
Larix occidentalis
Pine Family (Pinaceae)

Growth Form: Mature western larch reach 180 feet, with a remarkably straight trunk and narrow, pyramid-shaped crown. In older trees most branches are on the top portion of the tree. The bright green color of its foliage stands out against the darker green of surrounding conifers.

Bark: Older trees have deeply furrowed bark with cinnamon-colored scales. It is very thick near the base of the tree (4–6 inches) and can resist low- to moderate-intensity fire.

Bark

Cones: Cones are produced from May until June. Egg-shaped seed (female) cones are 1–1½ inches long and brown to reddish when mature. The cone scales are wider than they are long, and are loose and open. A long, narrow bract protrudes beyond each cone scale.

Needles: Soft and flexible, growing about 1½ inches long. Tufts of 15 to 30 needles are bundled at the tips of stubby twigs that radiate from the main branch. In cross section the needles are 3-sided. Needles are bright green in summer, turn brilliant yellow in autumn, then fall from the tree in early winter.

Needles and Cones

Habitat and Range: Western larch grows almost entirely near or west of the Continental Divide. It is common in mountain valleys and on lower slopes throughout western Montana, northern Idaho, and eastern Washington and Oregon. In Canada it grows in the interior mountains of southern British Columbia and southwestern Alberta.

Pests and Disease: Western larch is relatively free of disease and insect pests. The larch casebearer, an insect introduced from Europe in the late 1800's, infests all species of larch, except subalpine larch (*Larix lyallii*, pg. 38) in North America. Casebearer larvae feed on the inner tissue of larch needles, gradually defoliating the tree. Trees that experience perennial defoliation eventually succumb to the infestation. As with all dis-

Western Larch in Summer

eases, trees that are experiencing additional stress (i.e. drought, etc.) are particularly vulnerable. Dwarf mistletoe (pg. 23) is the most damaging disease-causing parasite of larch. It can infect seedlings as young as 3 to 7 years old and continue throughout the life of the tree, often killing the top.

Western Larch Fall Foliage

Notes: Larch depends on an open canopy and plenty of sun to survive and grow to great heights. It is one of the first trees to establish after a wildfire has burned through a forest. It grows fast in these conditions, and is often the tallest tree in a forest of mixed conifers. Once a forest has established and light to the forest floor is partially occluded, larch regeneration is minimal. Larch forests can produce heavy timber volumes. The wood is hard and used extensively for lumber, fine veneer, long-straight utility poles, railroad ties, mine timbers, and pulpwood. Lichen often establish on and hang from larch tree branches (lower photo, opposite page). Lichens flourish on larch limbs because they can photosynthesize during the late winter and spring, when the tree has no leaves. The largest western larch in the world occurs near the town of Seeley Lake, south of Glacier National Park.

Engelmann Spruce and White Spruce
Picea engelmannii and Picea glauca
Pine Family (Pinaceae)

Growth Form: Engelmann and white spruce are difficult to distinguish, and tend to interbreed, producing hybrid trees that bear characteristics intermediate between the two species. Engelmann spruce grows up to 165 feet tall at low- to mid-elevation and has a lush, pyramidal crown. Near treeline it is stunted and sometimes shrubby, forming "krummholz" stands on windswept slopes and ridges. White spruce is a smaller tree, reaching 60–80 feet, with a more conical crown.

Bark: Bark of mature spruce trees is thin and gray to reddish brown with shingle-like scales that pull easily from the tree.

Bark

Cones: Reddish purple seed cones are produced in spring, turning light brown as they mature in the fall. Each cone is 1–2½ inches long at maturity. Cones are plentiful in the upper portion of the crown. Examination of the cone scales is useful in differentiating between Engelmann and white spruce. The scales of Engelmann spruce are wider toward the base and have a jagged margin. Scales of white spruce are fan-shaped, wider toward the tip, and have a smooth, rounded margin.

Needles: Needles of both Engelmann and white spruce are distinctly sharp-pointed, stiff and prickly to the touch. They are about 1 inch long and spirally arranged, projecting from all sides of the twigs. The foliage is very aromatic when crushed.

Cones of White Spruce (left) and Engelmann Spruce

Habitat and Range: Engelmann spruce is a tree of cool, moist, mountainous habitats. Large, luxuriant trees are often found along streams and rivers, where cool air settles and moisture is plentiful. It is common in swampy forests and along streams in the montane zone, and on moist slopes at higher elevation. Engelmann spruce is widely distributed in the western United States and throughout the mountains of British Columbia and Alberta. Its range extends south from west central British Columbia along the eastern slope of the Coast Range in Washington, Oregon and northern California. It also extends along the crest and eastern slope of the Cascade Mountains through these states. In the interior northwest Engelmann spruce grows in mountain forests of Montana and Idaho, south to Arizona and New Mexico.

Needles and Open Cones

Engelmann Spruce

Habitat and Range (cont.): White spruce is common along streams and in swamp forests where water is near the soil surface throughout the year. It is a boreal plant, occurring at mostly low elevations across northern North America from Alaska to Quebec. In the United States it grows in the northern states, from Montana to Maine.

Pests and Disease: The Cooley spruce adelgid, a small, soft-bodied insect, frequently attacks Engelmann and white spruce resulting in the formation of pineapple-shaped, green galls that are often mistaken for cones. See page 25 for more information on this insect and its effect on northern forests. Spruce budworm (pg. 20) does occur on spruce, but seems to be more common on Douglas fir in the northern Rockies and Glacier National Park.

Notes: Spruce trees tend to be shallow-rooted, especially in wet areas. This character disposes them to wind throw, so the largest, oldest trees are more often found in upland habitats. Some sources indicate that hybridization between Engelmann and white spruce is so widespread that pure white spruce does not exist in Montana, including Glacier National Park. The hybrid is most likely found at lower elevations, while high-elevation trees are usually pure Engelmann spruce. Look for it mixed with subalpine fir in mountain forests and in patches of shrubby krummholz at treeline. Pure white spruce is more likely to be found at lower elevations in the mountains of Alberta and British Columbia. Seedlings of both species establish more readily in partial shade than in the open. Spruce lumber typically contains many small knots, so is most commonly used in making prefabricated wood products.

Whitebark Pine

Pinus albicaulis
Pine Family (Pinaceae)

Growth Form: Whitebark pine trees grow straight and erect in relatively moist, sheltered sites below timberline, where they reach heights up to 100 feet. In this environment trees usually have ascending rather than horizontal limbs. In exposed, high-elevation sites trees are shorter and often gnarled or twisted with multiple stems and a more open crown. In especially harsh sites the tree appears shrub-like and may be only 18 inches tall after decades of growth.

Bark: Bark of mature trees is light gray and scaly. Younger trees have smooth bark, also light gray in color.

Cones: Seed cones grow in clusters of 3 to 5 on the tips of upper branches. They are egg-shaped, reddish purple and 1½–3½ inches long. Intact cones are seldom observed on the ground because they are torn apart before they fall by Clark's nutcrackers, who enthusiastically harvest the seeds. Red squirrels also harvest whitebark pine cones, then cache dozens to hundreds of cones across the subalpine landscape. Bears raid these caches, thereby avoiding the necessity of climbing the trees to harvest whitebark pine seeds.

Bark

Needles: Bundled in groups of five, each needle is about 3 inches long. The foliage has a yellowish green hue compared to other subalpine trees, like subalpine fir (pg. 36).

Habitat and Range: Whitebark pine grows as a tree in subalpine forests throughout the Park. It also forms shrubby "krummholz" just above treeline. Its range includes British Columbia and western Alberta, extending south through Washington, Oregon, Idaho, Montana and Wyoming. Whitebark pine also grows in the mountains of northern and central California.

Needles and Cones

Pests and Disease: White pine blister rust has decimated the whitebark pine population across the northern Rocky Mountains. Once plentiful at high elevations, forests of whitebark pine have been replaced by "ghost forests" of dead trees due to the devastating effects of blister rust disease on this species. The life cycle of white pine blister rust is complex and fascinating, involving multiple hosts. See page 14 for a complete description of the blister rust disease cycle and a summary of historical attempts to control its spread. Mountain pine beetle infestations (pg. 17), climate change, and disrupted fire regimes have also negatively impacted whitebark pine survival in the last fifty years.

Whitebark Pine

Notes: Whitebark pine plays a crucial role in maintaining the health of subalpine ecosystems. It is considered a keystone species of the upper subalpine zone through-out the northern Rocky Mountains and Pacific Coastal ranges. A keystone species, similar to the keystone in an arch, has a disproportionate affect on its environment relative to its size or biomass. The large, fatty seeds of whitebark pine are dense sources of energy for many high-elevation forest inhabitants, including grizzly bear, black bear and many species of birds and small mammals. Elimination of whitebark pine from these ecosystems is widely thought to have devastating impacts on popula-tions of animals whose survival depends on these seeds.

Clark's nutcrackers are the primary agents of seed dispersal for whitebark pine, cach-ing hundreds of seeds in open, treeline habitats, then failing to return to the caches to retrieve the seeds. The forgotten seeds often germinate, producing multiple seedlings from one cache.

Lodgepole Pine
Pinus contorta
Pine Family (Pinaceae)

Growth Form: Lodgepole pine trees are remarkably straight, slender and relatively small in stature. In the montane zone they grow up to 100 ft tall; at higher elevation they are typically shorter and have a more compact growth form.

Bark: Bark of mature trees is light gray, scaly and thin. Individual scales are small and easily pried from the tree. The inner bark, observed on some trees where outer bark has cracked and separated, is reddish brown. Bark of saplings is also light gray, but smooth instead of scaly.

Bark

Cones: Seed cones are brown, egg-shaped and 1½–2 inches long. Each cone scale bears a prickly barb at the outer tip. Some of the cones are serotinous, an adaptation that enables them to quickly regenerate following a fire. The scales of serotinous cones are fused together and held by sticky sap, until they warm up and dry out in the sun, or are heated by a passing wildfire. Upon opening, the cones release hundreds of small, winged seeds.

Needles: Yellowish green and bundled together in groups of two. Lodgepole pine is the only 2-needled conifer in the northern Rockies. The needles are about 2 inches long.

Needles and Cones

Habitat and Range: Lodgepole pine trees often grow close to each other in densely crowded stands. These dense stands are more common at low- to mid-elevation, and develop as a result of a catastrophic fire that eliminated the forest previously occupying the site. At higher elevation, where wildfires are less frequent, trees are typically shorter and scattered across the landscape. Lodgepole pine grows throughout the western part of North America, from the Yukon south to California, Utah and Colorado.

Pests and Disease: Mountain pine beetle, a native of forests in western North America, frequently attack stands of lodgepole pine throughout the Rocky Mountains (pg. 17). Dense stands of older lodgepole pine trees are more susceptible to beetle infestations, primarily due to crowding. Closely spaced trees limit available resources, such as sunlight, for each tree. Our warming climate has made lodgepole pine particularly vulnerable to mountain pine beetle. Vast tracts of water-stressed lodgepole pine across our region are succumbing to infestations of this insect. Western gall rust and dwarf mistletoe (pg.23) also infect lodgepole pine throughout the Northern Rocky Mountains.

Lodgepole Pine Saplings Surrounding Mature Tree

Notes: There are four varieties of lodgepole pine. Our variety, var. *latifolia*, is the most eastern form, producing forests of straight, erect trees in the Rocky Mountains. Another variety, var. *contorta*, grows near sea level on the Pacific coast. The specific epithet *contorta* refers to this coastal form which has a bent growth form due to the prevailing westerly winds. Dense stands of lodgepole pine go through episodes of self-thinning which gradually reduces the density as plants in poor microsites perish from competition with their neighbors.

Lodgepole pine is well-known for its use as teepee poles by many Native tribes of the Rocky Mountains and northern plains. The straight, smooth trunks were also favored for building cabins and jack-leg fences by early European settlers. Decades of fire suppression has resulted in vast tracts of diseased and rotting forests of lodgepole pine. A variety of management techniques have been used to alleviate the problem, including harvesting of beetle-killed trees for commercial use, and the lighting of prescribed burns in an attempt to mimic the natural fire regime of these forests.

Limber Pine
Pinus flexilis
Pine Family (Pinaceae)

Growth Form: Limber pine is a slow-growing tree with a variable growth form that is strongly influenced by the environmental conditions of its habitat. At the lower end of its elevation range the tree has a stout, irregular trunk and many gnarled, ascending branches that form a rounded crown. Trees may have multiple stems. At higher elevations, where wind and weather make growing conditions more difficult, limber pine is shorter and even more gnarled. In the extremely harsh environment occurring at treeline the tree has a prostrate, shrubby growth form known as "krummholz."

Bark: Mature trees have scaly, light gray bark. The scales are irregularly oval in outline.

Bark

Cones: Immature seed cones are light green and require two seasons to mature. They turn brown and open toward the end of the second season. They are about 2–5 inches long and are produced on the branch tips. Unlike whitebark pine (pg. 44) cones, the cones of limber pine do not disintegrate on the tree. Instead, they dry out, open up, and often fall to the ground intact. Old trees may have a deep layer of old cones in various stages of decomposition at their base.

Female Cones

Needles: Yellowish-green needles are bundled in groups of five per fascicle. The needles are about 3 inches long.

Habitat and Range: In Glacier National Park, limber pine occupies dry, lowland slopes east of the Continental Divide, continuing up to treeline in some locations. It is most common on soils derived from limestone, but it may occur on sandstone- or quartzite-derived soils. Limber pine grows in the Rocky Mountains and intermountain ranges from southeastern British Columbia and southwestern Alberta to the northern portions of Arizona and New Mexico.

Needles and Male Cones

Limber Pine

Pests and Disease: Limber pine, like whitebark pine, has been severely impacted throughout its range by white pine blister rust. Tree seedlings infected with white pine blister rust entered North America from Europe in the early 1900's. The fungus gradually spread, infecting 5-needle pines across the United States. See page 14 for a more detailed description of the white pine blister rust disease cycle and attempts to control the spread of this fungus. Dwarf mistletoe (pg. 23) also impacts limber pine in some areas.

Notes: As with whitebark pine (pg. 44), Clark's nutcracker is an important disperser of limber pine seeds. Limber, whitebark and western white (pg. 50) pines are the only pine tree species with 5-needles per bundle growing in Glacier National Park. Limber pine and whitebark pine are difficult to differentiate, especially in seedling or sapling form. Mature, cone-producing trees can be distinguished by the presence or absence of cones under the tree. Intact limber pine cones are often present beneath mature trees; cones of whitebark pine are rarely observed beneath a tree because they are foraged upon by animals while still attached to the branch. Cone color and length may also be diagnostic. Limber pine cones are longer (5 inches) than those of white-bark pine (3½ inches), and are light green in early summer. Whitebark pine cones are reddish purple in early summer.

Western White Pine

Pinus monticola
Pine Family (Pinaceae)

Growth Form: Mature western white pine trees have straight, slender trunks and open crowns, and can grow up to 165 feet tall. These trees are intolerant of shade, so seedlings and saplings grow best in areas where sun can penetrate the canopy and reach the forest floor.

Bark: Bark of young trees is smooth and light gray. As trees mature the bark splits into scales, in a honeycomb-like pattern.

Bark

Cones: The seed cones of western white pine are distinctive, and a valuable aid in identifying this species. They are long (6–10 inches), slightly curved and dangle from up-per tree branches. Cone scales are loose and open. Cones fall to the ground intact, so can usually be observed on the ground beneath the tree.

Needles: Blue-green needles are 2–4 inches long and bundled in groups of five. They are distinctly soft and flexible.

Habitat and Range: Western white pine grows in moist, low- to mid-elevation forests west of the Conti-nental Divide in Glacier National Park and surrounding areas. It is typically

Needles and Cones

a component of a mixed-conifer forest, scattered among Douglas fir, grand fir, and/ or western hemlock. Western white pine occurs in the Coast, Cascade and Sierra Nevada mountain ranges of British Columbia, Washington, Oregon and California. It also grows in the Rocky Mountains from Alberta south through northern Idaho and northwest Montana.

Pests and Disease: Western white pine populations have been decimated by the spread of white pine blister rust, imported from Europe in the early 1900's on orna-mental white pine trees. Infestations of mountain pine beetle, a native of forests in western North America, have also affected this species. See page 14 for a detailed discussion of white pine blister rust, and page 17 for information on recent increases in mountain pine beetle infestations. The U.S. Forest Service has been actively en-gaged in selecting strains of this valuable tree that are resistant to blister rust.

Western White Pine

Notes: Whitebark pine (pg. 44) and limber pine (pg. 48) are two other 5-needle pines common in the northern Rockies. Western white pine needles are very different from these two species in color, length and texture. The needles of western white pine are considerably longer and softer than those of whitebark or limber pine. The blue-green color of western white pine foliage and this tree's distinctive banana-shaped cones also differentiate it from the other two species. Due to their size, cones growing high in the crown are easily visible from ground level.

This species has been highly prized as a commercial tree. Its long, straight trunk and lightweight, nonresinous, straight-grained wood have made it the most valuable tree for lumber in Montana and adjacent Idaho. However, between harvest and disease there are few large trees left except in protected areas such as Glacier National Park. The relatively thin bark and moderately flammable foliage make western white pine intermediate in fire resistance among conifers. Nonetheless sun-loving western white pine depends on fire for its own successful establishment. It's the State Tree of Idaho; the world's largest western white pine is found in the northern part of that state.

Ponderosa Pine
Pinus ponderosa
Pine Family (Pinaceae)

Growth Form: Mature ponderosa pine trees have a rounded crown with spreading branches and may reach up to 165 feet in height.

Bark: The bark of young ponderosa pines is dark and has a bumpy texture. As the tree matures the bark becomes orange-brown in color, and irregular-shaped plates develop. The plates are easily "chipped" from the tree and resemble jigsaw puzzle pieces. The ground beneath large trees sometimes looks piled up with pieces from many jigsaw puzzles. On a hot summer day, when the bark is warmed by the sun, it has a pleasant vanilla scent.

Bark

Cones: Oblong, purplish seed cones are produced on branch tips. They are broadly oval-shaped, 3–6 inches long, and require two growing seasons to mature. Cones fall to the ground intact, and are often scattered under trees. Cone scales open as the cones dry, exposing sharp prickles on the tips of scales. This character makes handling the cones with bare hands difficult. Clark's nutcrackers and small mammals harvest the seeds and cache those that they do not consume. Forgotten caches of seeds often germinate, enhancing seed dispersal for this species.

Needles: Yellowish-green and 5–8 inches long. They are bundled in groups of three (occasionally two) and clustered toward the ends of branches. Older trees typically have a deep layer of brown, shed needles around the tree base.

Needles and Female Cones

Habitat and Range: In Glacier National Park ponderosa pine is confined to areas along the Park's western boundary, bordering grasslands along the North Fork of the Flathead River. Outside the Park, in areas with warm, dry summers, it may be the dominant tree in open woodlands or bordering grasslands. It is rare east of the Continental Divide, north of the Dearborn River. Ponderosa pine grows in the Rocky Mountains from British Columbia and Alberta to Arizona and New Mexico. It is also common in the Cascade Mountains of Washington and Oregon, and the Sierra Nevada Range of California.

Male Cones

Ponderosa Pine

Pests and Disease: Western gall rust is a fungus infecting 2- and 3-needle pines across the United States, forming globe-shaped galls (swellings) on tree branches and occasionally on trunks. Infection occurs when airborne fungal spores penetrate new shoots, moving into the succulent tissue of young branches. Mountain pine beetles (see pg. 17) have also impacted this species, decimating many stands in southwestern Montana.

Notes: Ponderosa pine trees are intolerant of shade, which makes them highly dependent on frequent, low-intensity fire. Low-intensity fire keeps more shade-tolerant species, such as grand and Douglas fir, from establishing and eventually overtaking the habitat of ponderosa pine. It also kills younger ponderosa pine. Fire suppression has made open, healthy ponderosa pine woodlands an uncommon sight. Forests dominated by large ponderosa pines now are often choked with saplings that are able to survive without periodic ground fire. Basal fire scars are common on the thick-barked stems of old-growth trees. Ponderosa pine is the State Tree of Montana. Trees from mountainous regions generally have needles in bundles of three, while those found on the Great Plains have mainly two needles per bundle.

Douglas Fir
Pseudotsuga menziesii
Pine Family (Pinaceae)

Growth Form: Mature Douglas fir trees have a pyramidal shaped crown with spreading to drooping branches and can grow up to 170 feet tall. Trees growing on steep slopes often have a J-shaped lower trunk, sometimes called a "pistol butt."

Bark: Mature trees have grayish, corky bark with reddish brown furrows. Bark of younger trees is gray and smooth with scattered resin blisters. Thick bark makes Douglas fir very resistant to fire, surpassed in this regard only by ponderosa pine and western larch. In relatively moist habitats low-intensity fire favors Douglas fir by removing less fire-resistant species, such as spruce and true fir.

Bark

Cones: Seed cones are brown, cylindrical and 1½–2½ inches long. The rounded cone scales have a 3-tipped bract that protrudes from each cone scale. The bract resembles the protruding legs and tail of a tiny squirrel diving head-first into each cone scale.

Needles: Yellowish-green to bluish-green. Needles grow from all sides of the branch, giving twigs a bottlebrush appearance. Individual needles are flattened, not sharp to the touch, and have two white stripes on the lower surface.

Habitat and Range: Douglas fir is abundant throughout the Northern Rockies in all mid-elevation forests. It can tolerate a wide range of environmental stress, including drought and low-intensity fire. Vast tracts of Douglas fir for-

Needles and Cones

ests exist on the west side of the Continental Divide in Glacier National Park. East of the Divide in the Park, forests dominated by Douglas fir are common in the St. Mary Valley. Douglas fir grows throughout the western part of North America, from Alberta and British Columbia through California, Arizona and New Mexico. Isolated populations also occur in Mexico.

Pests and Disease: Western spruce budworms (pg. 20) attack Douglas fir, grand fir, subalpine fir, spruce and larch, but seem to have the most adverse effects on Douglas fir. Budworm caterpillars damage trees by feeding on needle and shoot growth in the spring, then pupating (entering an inactive stage) elsewhere on the tree or on the ground nearby. Subsequent years of defoliation can cause dieback of tree branches and crown. Outbreaks of spruce budworm are usually cyclical, giving trees time to recover between outbreaks. However, recent outbreaks have been long-lived and resulted in some mortality. Douglas fir is also prone to mistletoe infestations (pg. 23) throughout its range, especially where trees are crowded.

Douglas Fir

Notes: Our trees are var. *glauca*, a variety of this species that is adapted to relatively dry conditions. Moist sites of the Pacific slope support var. *menziesii*. In Montana Douglas fir is particularly common on limestone. Douglas fir is the timber industry's most widely used species. It is not a "true fir" like grand and subalpine firs. Its name reflects the initial confusion botanists experienced in classifying this unique tree. Young trees bear resin blisters like true firs, yet its needles resemble other species, such as spruce and yew. Ultimately the tree was given its own genus, *Pseudotsuga*, translated as "false-hemlock," reflecting its similarity to yet another tree species. Only one other *Pseudotsuga* is recognized in the western hemisphere: bigcone Douglas fir (*Pseudotsuga macrocarpa*), a smaller species that occupies southern mountain ranges of California. Fire suppression has allowed Douglas fir to invade many areas previously dominated by grasslands.

Western Hemlock
Tsuga heterophylla
Pine Family (Pinaceae)

Growth Form: Mature western hemlock trees have a pyramidal crown and drooping branches. The leader, visible at the top of the crown, arches gracefully downward, and the foliage appears feathery from a distance. Trees growing in and around Glacier National Park typically reach around 130 feet at maturity.

Bark: Bark of mature trees is brown, thin and scaly. Shallow, vertical furrows are scattered across the trunk, dividing the bark into long, slender plates. Its thin bark makes trees very susceptible to fires, which occur only rarely in hemlock's rainy habitat.

Bark

Cones: Seed cones are plentiful throughout the canopy of trees as young as 25 years. They are green when first produced, turning brown when they mature. The cones are about an inch long and oval in outline. Cone scales are open and papery. Each scale bears a small, winged seed. The ground beneath a mature western hemlock tree is typically littered with cones. Cones require only one growing season to mature.

Needles: Western hemlock needles are distinctly soft, flexible and light green in color. They are flat in cross-section and vary in length from ¼–¾ inch. Needles are arranged along the branch in a single plane, or nearly so. Each needle has two white bands of stomata on the lower surface, appearing as two stripes that run the length of the needle.

Needles and Cones

Habitat and Range: Western hemlock prefers moist to wet, shady forests. Seedlings readily establish on rotting logs lying on the forest floor. Western hemlock is very shade tolerant and has no problem growing under the canopy of Douglas fir and larch if the climate is moist enough. In Glacier Park western hemlock often occurs with western red cedar (pg. 32). Western hemlock primarily grows along the coast from southern Alaska to northern California. It also occurs in the Rocky Mountains of British Columbia, western Alberta, northern Idaho and northwest Montana.

Pests and Disease: Western hemlock has not been impacted by significant pests or disease in Glacier National Park or surrounding areas. Root rot is common in old-growth trees, but rarely causes mortality. Deer and elk are known to browse the foliage during winter.

Western Hemlock

Notes: Western hemlock trees usually establish in the shady understory of mature forests. They require significant moisture and are very sensitive to disturbance caused by fire or timber harvest. Because of these characters, western hemlock's distribution is limited in the northern Rockies. It is plentiful in the McDonald Valley of Glacier National Park, and moist forests of northern Idaho. Western hemlock is the State Tree of Washington.

A similar species, mountain hemlock (*T. mertensiana*, pg. 58), occurs near Glacier National Park. Its needles are bluish-green and produced on all sides of the branch or twig, in a bottlebrush arrangement, and its cones are much longer.

Mountain Hemlock
Tsuga mertensiana
Pine Family (Pinaceae)

Growth Form: Mountain hemlock is a rugged tree with a full canopy and narrowly pyramidal crown. Like western hemlock (previous page) its leader arches gracefully downward and its foliage appears feathery from a distance.

Bark: Mature trees have dark brown to purplish brown bark with deep, vertical fissures. The bark is a little over an inch thick.

Cones: Oblong seed cones hang like pendulums from upper branches. They are dark purple when young, turning medium brown at maturity, and 1½–3 inches long.

Bark

Needles: Produced on all sides of the branch or twig, in a bottlebrush arrangement and ½–¾ inch long. The foliage has a bluish tint, in contrast to that of western hemlock, which has a yellowish green hue.

Habitat and Range: Mountain hemlock occupies moist, snowy, sheltered sites. It has a relatively limited distribution in the northern Rocky Mountains of northwest Montana, northern Idaho and southern British Columbia. Although it does not occur in Glacier National Park, it occurs south of the Park in the Mission Mountains, and southwest of the Park in the Cabinet Mountains. Its range extends from the coast of southeastern Alaska to Washington. It occurs in the Coast and Cascade Ranges of the Pacific Northwest, and the Rocky Mountains of Idaho and Montana. Populations of mountain hemlock are also scattered in the Sierra Nevada Mountains of California.

Cones

Pests and Disease: Mountain hemlock has no significant pests and disease in our area.

Needles

Notes: Mountain hemlock cones are much longer than those of western hemlock (pg 56). They resemble Engelmann spruce cones (pg. 42) more than those of western hemlock. The needle arrangement of mountain hemlock is also different than that of western hemlock. The needles of western hemlock are produced in rows on either side of the twig and are arranged in flattened sprays.

Mountain Hemlock

Notes (cont.): Mountain hemlock is abundant in western mountain ranges near the coast, where moisture is plentiful and temperatures are more moderate. In Montana it is most common along the Idaho Divide where snow lies late into the summer. It is thought that mountain hemlock cannot tolerate frozen soil so it is found only in areas with deep layers of insulating snow cover throughout the winter. This species is shade-tolerant, regenerating easily under the canopies of other trees. Early Americans used the boughs of mountain hemlock as sleeping mats.

Water Birch
Betula occidentalis
Birch Family (Betulaceae)

Growth form: Water birch is a tree or tall shrub growing with multiple, tightly clumped stems. Occasionally it will produce a single, more robust stem. Its height ranges from 20–45 feet.

Bark: Dull gray to dark brown with very little peeling. Small, horizontal marks scattered across the trunk are called lenticels. They are pores that allow gas exchange between the atmosphere and the inner tissues of the trunk. The bark of twigs has small, widely scattered glands that exude a bit of sticky resin.

Bark

Catkins: Two types of catkins, male and female, are produced on the same tree. Male catkins are long and pendulous. They are produced in clusters of 2 or more. Female catkins are cone-shaped to cylindrical and ¾–1½ inches long. They point upward. Female catkins disintegrate at maturity.

Leaves: Oval in outline, but with one end obviously narrowed (ovate). Leaf tips may be blunt or slightly pointed, and the margins are sharply toothed. The length varies from ¾–2 inches. Young leaves have a glandular, slightly sticky texture and are sparsely white-hairy beneath.

Leaves and Male Catkins

Habitat and Range: Water birch is found almost exclusively in riparian habitats, along streams and rivers, and near seeps. It occurs throughout the inland west of Canada and the United States, extending from the Yukon Territory south, to the mountainous parts of Arizona and New Mexico. It is less common on the western sides of the Cascade and Coastal mountain ranges.

Pests and Disease: Water birch has no serious insect or disease pests in our area. However, it is shallow-rooted and prone to drought injury and wind throw. Both water and paper birch (*Betula papyrifera*, page 32) are relatively short-lived trees; most trees die well before they're 100 years old.

Water Birch

Notes: The common name, water birch, is indicative of this tree's strong affinity for wet sites. It is sometimes called river birch, or black birch due to the color of its bark. Its species name, *occidentalis*, means "western" and refers to its primary distribution. In Glacier National Park, look for water birch in shrubby thickets along the Middle Fork of the Flathead River, and bordering streams that drain from lakes on both sides of the Continental Divide.

Paper Birch
Betula papyrifera
Birch Family (Betulaceae)

Growth Form: Paper birch grows as a single-stemmed tree or cluster of 2 to 5 stems up to 50 feet tall. Taller trees may be found growing in open areas with especially fertile soil.

Bark: Color of young tree bark ranges from gray to brown. Mature tree bark is white to yellowish and peels away from the stem in sheets. Some paper birch trees may be darker colored with little peeling, due to hybridization with water birch (*Betula occidentalis*, see Notes). The bark of twigs is sparsely covered with fine hair and tiny glands, making some twigs slightly sticky to the touch.

Bark

Catkins: Male and female catkins are produced on the same tree. Female catkins hang downward like a pendulum and are scattered along branches. They are about ¾–2 inches long and disintegrate when mature. Male catkins elongate in the spring and also hang like long pendulums. They are produced in clusters of 2 or more.

Leaves and Female Catkins

Leaves: Oval in outline, but with one end obviously narrowed (ovate). The narrowed end tapers abruptly to form concave sides, then a sharp leaf tip. The leaf margins are coarsely toothed. The length of the leaf blade ranges from 2–3 inches. Tiny patches of rust-brown hair are produced at some of the vein junctions on the underside of leaf blades.

Habitat and Range: Paper birch is scattered throughout moist forests in the lower montane zones of the Park, and in open areas where the soil stays fairly moist. It is common in forests across northern North America. Its range reaches from near the Pacific coast in British Columbia, Washington and Oregon to coastal New England and southeast Canada.

Male Catkins

Pests and Disease: The paper birch population in the US and Canada has been severely impacted by the bronze birch borer. This small beetle, native to North America, apparently prefers white-barked species of birch over species with darker bark. See pg. 27 for more information on how bronze birch borers infect and kill birch trees.

Paper Birch

Notes: The bark of this tree was used in the construction of birchbark canoes by Native Americans and early settlers. Cedar canoe frames were covered with sheets of bark, carefully sown together, to make these lightweight boats. Hybridization with water birch (*Betula occidentalis*, pg. 61) is relatively common, producing trees with characteristics of both species. Plants intermediate between water birch and paper birch occur west of the Continental Divide. These plants have peeling gray bark, nearly glandless twigs and sparse hair on the underside of the leaves.

Russian Olive
Elaeagnus angustifolia
Oleaster Family (Elaeagnaceae)

Growth Form: This silvery-green, spreading tree or tall shrub grows up to 25 feet. Trees that have established in open sites with fertile soil may grow taller and become more robust and have a rounded crown. In riparian areas and moist meadows its growth form is shrubby and it may form thickets.

Bark: Mature trees have grooved bark, gray in color and peeling in strips. The bark of young branches is silvery.

Flowers and Fruit: Russian olive produces clusters of creamy yellow flowers among its leaves at branch tips. Flowers have four spreading lobes that are united into a tube at the flower base. They are fragrant and produced in May to early June. Its berry-like fruit are silvery-gray, egg-shaped and about ½ inch long. They are widest near the tip.

Leaves: Its dull, silvery-green leaves are lance shaped and 2–3 inches long. The branches bear sharp-tipped thorns.

Flowers and Leaves

Habitat and Range: Russian olive is extremely adaptable, growing in open meadows and along river corridors. It is now reported as invasive in almost all of the United States. It is most problematic in the Great Basin Desert and in riparian areas of the Great Plains.

Pests and Disease: Russian olive has very hard wood and few insect pests. As a result, stands of Russian olive support few insectivorous or cavity-nesting birds compared to our native cottonwood and willow. Russian olive has a symbiotic relationship with a nitrogen-fixing fungus that enables it to produce dense wood and still grow quickly.

Fruit

Russian Olive

Notes: Russian olive is native to southern Europe, and to western and central Asia. Hardy trees were brought to this country and planted by Menonites in South Dakota, where they readily established and spread into eastern Montana. It is often planted as a hedge, windbreak or snowbreak in windy zones east of the Continental Divide. In the northern Rocky Mountains Russian olive is sometimes used as an ornamental shade tree. It is well adapted to milder climates but rarely occurs above our mountain foothills. Once established, it is very drought tolerant, and will sprout from the base after being damaged or cut. The tree has become a considerable problem in some areas, where its vigorous growth has displaced native cottonwoods along river corridors. Its dense foliage reduces light to the understory, inhibiting establishment of native trees and other plant species.

Black Cottonwood

Populus trichocarpa or P. balsamifera ssp. trichocarpa
Willow Family (Salicaceae)

Growth Form: Black cottonwood is a deciduous tree growing up to 130 feet tall. Its crown is column-shaped and dense with leaves. Smaller trees often sprout from the roots of a mature tree.

Bark: Saplings have smooth, white bark that cracks as the tree ages. Bark of mature trees is gray, thick and deeply furrowed.

Bark

Flowers and Fruit: Black cottonwood produces male and female flowers on separate trees. Female flowers are arranged in tightly clustered spikes of flowers, called catkins, that lack true petals and sepals. Black cottonwood catkins hang from twigs and are 3–8 inches long. Female flowers mature into capsules that hang in clusters like small, green grapes. The capsules split open in early to mid-summer to release tiny seeds that are adorned with a tuft of fluffy, cotton-like hair. The downy hair enables seeds to travel great distances in the wind.

Flowers

Leaves: Broadly lance-shaped and 1½–5½ inches long. They are arranged alternately along the twigs. The upper surface is dark green, while the lower surface is silvery white to very pale green. Leaf margins are toothed and the tip narrows abruptly to a point. Leaves turn deep yellow in autumn. Expanding leaves in spring are coated with a brown, aromatic resin that can fill the air with a spicy odor on a warm day.

Habitat and Range: Black cottonwood is abundant along rivers and streams throughout the Rocky Mountains. It also occurs in moist forests and avalanche chutes, and on the shores of mountain lakes. The farther north one goes the more often this species can be found in upland habitats such as aspen groves and on cool mountain slopes. Its range extends from Alaska south to California, and east to North Dakota, Wyoming and Utah.

Leaves and Fruit

Pests and Disease: Old trees may develop cankers due to fungal infection, but the condition is rarely fatal for the tree. Woodpeckers forage for insects in the cracks of black cottonwood bark, sometimes causing scars. Beavers use these trees for dams and lodges, and will cut down trees growing 10–20 feet from a river channel.

Black Cottonwood in Fall

Notes: Groves of black cottonwood create stunning displays along river corridors in spring as they unfurl their bright green leaves, and in autumn when their leaves turn beautiful shades of yellow and gold. A new grove of cottonwood seedlings often emerges when fresh gravel bars are created by a river's dynamic movement across a floodplain. Hundreds of seeds might germinate in one season, initiating a stand of trees the same age and size. These uniform stands of black cottonwood grow on floodplain terraces along the Middle Fork Flathead River, which makes up a large portion of Glacier's southwestern boundary. In spite of its thick bark, even old black cottonwood trees are highly susceptible to fire. Black cottonwood or balsam poplar can be seen mixed with aspen in many groves on the east side of Glacier National Park. Trees are host to a diversity of insects that attract many insectivorous birds and bats.

Quaking Aspen
Populus tremuloides
Willow Family (Salicaceae)

Growth Form: Quaking aspen is a deciduous, broad-leaved tree growing up to 100 feet tall. Mature trees have dome-shaped crowns, dense with leaves that tremble in the slightest breeze. Trees at low-elevation grow tall with straight trunks. In the subalpine zone trees are typically stunted and may have gnarled, twisted stems.

Bark

Bark: Mature trees have smooth, white bark with black marks of various size and shape. The bark of saplings is light green and smooth. Bark on the lower portion of very old, large trees often cracks and darkens.

Flowers and Fruit: Male and female flowers are produced on separate trees. The flowers are arranged in catkins, tightly clustered spikes of flowers that lack true petals and sepals. Female catkins hang from twigs and are 1½–4 inches long. Minute seeds are released in early summer. They are covered in fluff, which helps them drift long distances in the wind.

Female Catkins

Leaves: Aspen leaves are nearly round in outline. They are green on the upper leaf surface, pale on the underside, and have scalloped margins with an abruptly pointed tip. The leaf stalk (petiole) is thin and flat in cross-section, allowing the blade to turn with the slightest air movement.

Habitat and Range: Aspen occupies sites on both sides of the Continental Divide in Glacier National Park, but is more common to the east, where it forms extensive groves of similar-aged trees in moist depressions or on cool slopes. Aspen occurs across Canada and the United States, with the exception of the southeastern States.

Leaves

Pests and Disease: There are no significant diseases or pests affecting quaking aspen populations in and around Glacier National Park. Outside the Park, aspen have been impacted by the poplar borer (lower photo), which lays eggs on aspen bark. Beetle larvae tunnel into the trunk and weaken it by feeding on the wood. Fungi can readily establish in entry and exit holes, further weakening the tree.

Poplar Borer Exit Hole

Quaking Aspen in Fall

Pests and Disease (cont.): When small limbs die they leave a weakened area on the trunk that is easily excavated by woodpeckers and other cavity-nesting birds. Aspens are fed on by many insects, especially moth caterpillars that in turn feed many insectivorous birds.

Notes: Quaking aspen is sometimes called "trembling aspen." The flattened petiole allows the leaves to quiver easily, which produces a distinctive rustling sound when moved by the slightest breeze. Aspens form large colonies by sending up shoots from horizontally-spreading roots. Some aspen clones have been shown to be more than a thousand years old. Clones often initiate following fire. They can be reduced or even killed by browsing of young sprouts or shading by taller-growing conifers that manage to establish with the aspen. Aspen has a stunted growth form in areas of high wind and severe winter weather. The tree bark contains salicin, a compound known to alleviate pain and reduce inflammation. Northern Native American tribes used a tea made from aspen bark to treat a variety of ailments, including diarrhea, infections and skin problems.

Narrow-leaved Cottonwood
Populus angustifolia
Willow Family (Salicaceae)

Growth Form: Narrow-leaved cottonwood is a slender, deciduous tree growing up to 70 feet tall at maturity.

Bark: Young trees have smooth, yellowish green bark. As the tree matures the bark turns gray-green and develops shallow, scattered furrows.

Flowers and Fruit: Female catkins are produced in early summer. Catkins are 2–3 inches long and are made up of a cluster of green, oval capsules, resembling tiny, green grapes. The capsules contain tiny seeds, each with a tuft of hair that enables the seed to drift easily in the wind.

Leaves: True to its name, the leaves of narrow-leaved cottonwood are long and narrow. They are much narrower than our other common cottonwood, black cottonwood (pg. 66). Leaves are 2–4 inches long and are 3 to 5 times longer than they are wide. The petiole (leaf stalk) is relatively short. Its length is less than a third of the length of the leaf blade.

Leaves

Habitat and Range: Narrow-leaved cottonwood occupies moist riparian sites at low- to mid-elevation. It is frequently observed along rivers and streams. In the northern Rockies narrow-leaved cottonwood is common in southern Alberta, Montana and Idaho. Its range continues south to California, Arizona, New Mexico and Texas.

Notes: Narrow-leaved cottonwood is far less common in the northern Rocky Mountains than black cottonwood. It has not been documented within the boundaries of Glacier National Park, but occurs just south of the Park along the Rocky Mountain Front, and east of the Park on the Blackfeet Indian Reservation. Narrow-leaved cottonwood dominates riparian corridors along the Yellowstone River, above Livingston, Montana. It is the most common native cottonwood growing along streams and rivers in Utah.

Narrow-leaved Cottonwood

Crack Willow
Salix fragilis
Willow Family (Salicaceae)

Growth Form: Crack willow is a medium-sized tree that reaches a maximum height of 65 feet at maturity. Young trees have a conical growth form. The crown of mature trees is more rounded, especially if growing in an open area.

Bark: Bark of young trees is gray and scaly. As the tree matures, cracks develop in the bark, becoming deeper over time. Mature trees have grayish brown, fissured bark.

Bark

Flowers and Fruit: Male and female catkins are produced on different trees. Male catkins are yellowish and 1½–3 inches long. Female catkins are about the same size, bearing light green capsules, which split open in July to release seeds.

Leaves: Young leaves are hairy on both the top and bottom surfaces. As they elongate the hair is lost, and leaves become shiny and smooth on the upper surface, and bluish-green on the lower surface. At maturity the leaves are 2–5 inches long and finely serrated along the margin.

Leaves and Female Catkins

Habitat and Range: Crack willow is common along river corridors and other moist places at low-elevation. It occurs across Canada from Alberta to Newfoundland. In the United States its range extends from Washington east to Maine, and south to Utah, New Mexico, Missouri and Virginia.

Male Catkins

Crack Willow

Notes: Crack willow was originally introduced to North America from Europe by settlers who used it for shade and as an ornamental. It has naturalized across the United States, into the northern Rocky Mountains. Many of these trees are actually hybrids with white willow (*Salix alba*), another willow imported by Europeans. The common name "crack willow" refers to the brittle nature of this plant's twigs. They break easily, producing an audible snap. The broken twigs readily root in moist soil, producing dense stands of young crack willow trees along rivers and streams. While this species has not been documented in Glacier National Park, it is common just south of the Park, in Flathead and Mission Valleys.

Peachleaf Willow
Salix amygdaloides
Willow Family (Salicaceae)

Growth Form: Peachleaf willow is a small tree or tall shrub that reaches a maximum height of about 40 feet at maturity. It has a single-stemmed or multi-stemmed growth form.

Bark: Bark of mature trees is thick, rough, yellowish gray to dark gray and covered with fissures.

Bark

Flowers and Fruit: Male and female catkins, produced on separate trees, are 1–3 inches long. Male catkins are yellowish and composed of densely clustered pollen-producing flowers. Female catkins are made up of stalked capsules and are light green. The capsules split open in July to release tiny, fluff-covered seeds.

Leaves: Mature leaves are smooth, hairless and yellowish green on the upper surface. The lower leaf surface has a thin, waxy coating, called a glaucous bloom, that is easily wiped away. Leaf length is 1–4 inches. Vigorous shoots may produce slightly longer leaves.

Leaves

Habitat and Range: Peachleaf willow occupies water courses and floodplains in low- to mid-elevation valleys and mountain foothills. It also grows along prairie waterways, where it is often the largest tree. It is native to North America, and frequently grows with black cottonwood (pg. 66) along major rivers at low-elevation. In Canada its range extends from British Columbia to Quebec, primarily growing in the southern portion of these provinces. In the United States it occurs from Washington and Oregon east to New York and Pennsylvania, and south to Arizona, Texas and Kentucky.

Female Catkins

Peachleaf Willow

Notes: Peachleaf willow is uncommon in Glacier National Park and the surrounding valleys. It occurs along the Middle Fork of the Flathead River, near West Glacier. It is more common on the Great Plains of eastern Montana and adjacent prairies. Peachleaf willow primarily regenerates by seed, rather than by rooting twigs like many other willows. It produces thousands of tiny seeds that are easily carried by wind and water to a suitable site for germination and establishment.

The Northern Cheyenne Tribe of Montana used peachleaf willow extensively for its medicinal properties, and as a building material. A tea made from the bark of this tree was used to treat intestinal ailments. They also applied a poultice of the bark to wounds, to stop bleeding. Willow boughs were used to build sweat lodges, and were bound together with sinew to create backrests.

Many species of insects, including caterpillars, mites and beetles feed on willow leaves and support a large number of insectivorous birds such as warblers and fly-catchers.

European Mountain Ash
Sorbus aucuparia
Rose Family (Rosaceae)

Growth Form: European mountain ash grows up to 33 feet tall and has a full, rounded to conical crown. It was introduced from Europe as an ornamental planting. It resembles its shrubby, native relatives, western mountain ash (pg. 111) and sitka mountain ash, but is distinctly more tree-like at maturity.

Bark: Mature trees have brownish gray bark with fissures at the base. Bark of younger trees is gray, sometimes appearing silvery gray, with scattered horizontal slits.

Flowers and Fruit: Flat-topped clusters of creamy-white flowers are produced in June. They have an unpleasant smell. Each flower has 5 petals and is about ½ inch across. Berries form in July, changing color from green to bright red as the season progresses.

Leaves: Leaves grow in an alternate arrangement along the twigs. They are divided into 13 to 15 lance-shaped leaflets. Leaflets are smooth and hairless on the upper surface, and toothed along the margins. Each leaflet is ¾–2 inches long. They turn bright red in the fall.

Habitat and Range: European ash establishes in sites with relatively moist and mild climatic conditions. In the Park there are scattered trees in the McDonald Valley, along lower McDonald Creek. It has been used in landscaping across the US.

Notes: This tree has naturalized into low-elevation Rocky Mountain forests. It is also known as "rowan tree." Many bird species feast on the ripened fruits in the fall, particularly waxwings. Birds spread the seeds of European mountain ash by feeding on them in urban areas, then depositing them in nearby native forest. Cooked, sweetened fruit has been used in pies, jams and wine.

Flowers

Leaves and Fruit

Fall Color

European Mountain Ash

Common Juniper
Juniperus communis
Cedar Family (Cupressaceae)

Description: Spreading, evergreen shrub growing up to 3¼ feet tall. Its leaves are stiff, sharply pointed and needle-like, borne in whorls of three. They are dark green above and whitish on the lower surface. The leaves are jointed where they meet the stem. Male and female cones occur on separate plants. Seed cones, on female plants, resemble berries. They take two years to ripen and are green the first year, turning purplish-brown the second year.

Habitat and Range: Common juniper occurs in dry forest on exposed sites. It often grows in Douglas fir or lodgepole pine woodlands, or on rock outcrops. Its range extends across North America from Alaska to Greenland, south to Arizona, New Mexico, Kentucky and Virginia.

Notes: Juniper "berries" are edible. The darker, older berries are typically more flavorful. They are used to give gin its distinctive flavor, and to season meat. The Blackfeet Tribe used a liniment made by infusing juniper root and poplar leaves to alleviate back pain. They also drank a strong tea made from the root to promote over-all nutritional health. Modern-day herbalists use juniper as a diuretic and to dissolve kidney stones. Evening grosbeaks and cedar waxwings eat the berries.

Creeping Juniper
Juniperus horizontalis
Cedar Family (Cupressaceae)

Description: Low-growing, evergreen shrub with spreading, horizontal branches, stringy bark and aromatic foliage. Its leaves are scale-like, flattened and grow opposite each other along branches. Pairs of leaves occur so closely that they overlap. The leaf margins are entire (not toothed) and the leaf tip ends abruptly in a small, sharp point. The foliage is bright green to bluish green with a fine, waxy coating. Male and female cones are produced on separate plants. Female (seed) cones are composed of 3 to 8 fleshy, fused scales, appearing berry-like. They are initially green, turning bluish-black at maturity and about ¼ inch in diameter.

Habitat and Range: Creeping juniper is common on exposed ridges and grasslands along the eastern side of the Continental Divide in Glacier National Park. It often grows in rocky soil on shale slopes, and occasionally occurs above treeline. Its range includes Alaska, Canada, and most of the northern United States, with the exception of Oregon, Washington and Idaho.

Notes: Creeping juniper has been used extensively in the horticultural trade. It is a hardy plant, relatively deer resistant, and very attractive with its blue-green foliage. Native Americans used juniper berries to treat pain and respiratory problems, and to alleviate cold symptoms. Modern-day herbalists use the oil from pressed juniper berries as a tonic to promote general well-being. It has diuretic properties and is sometimes prescribed for detoxifying the digestive and urinary systems.

Yew
Taxus brevifolia
Yew Family (Taxaceae)

Description: Evergreen shrub to small tree growing up to 17 feet tall. Its branches are widespread and drooping. The bark of younger plants is thin and brown- to purple-colored. On older trees the bark is scaly, flaking in places to reveal an under-layer that is reddish brown. The leaves are ½–1 inch long and needle-like with a sharply pointed tip. They are deep green on the upper surface and have a raised midrib. The lower leaf surface is paler than the upper surface. The leaves grow opposite each other along twigs, in flat sprays. Male and female cones are produced on separate plants. Male cones are small, round and orange- to brown-colored. Female cones are composed of a single seed surrounded by a fleshy, berry-like cup (aril), about ½ inch in diameter. The aril is initially green, turning red at maturity.

Aril

Habitat and Range: Yew is common in the Park's montane forests on the west side of the Continental Divide. It occurs east of the Divide but is rare. It often forms dense thickets in the understory of old-growth forests. Its range extends from British Columbia and Alberta south to California. It also occurs in the southern portion of the Alaska Panhandle.

Notes: Yew is usually restricted to the understory of old forests that have been protected from fire. It is slow-growing, requires shady conditions, and easily killed by fire. Yew was used extensively by many Native American tribes as medicine. A strong tea made from the leaves was reported to speed healing of lung problems and internal injury, and alleviate pain. A poultice of the leaves was applied to burns and other skin lesions. Taxol, a compound found in yew bark, received significant recognition in the early 1990s for its ability to slow or even stop the growth of some cancers. Crews of harvesters made their way through thousands of acres, cutting yew trees, stripping their bark, and selling it to pharmaceutical processers. The pharmaceutical industry has since created synthetic forms of taxol, which are used to treat several types of cancer, including those of the neck, breast and ovaries.

Sitka Alder
Alnus viridis
Birch Family (Betulaceae)

Description: Deciduous shrub growing up to 10 feet high with arching, widespread branches and grayish bark. The young twigs are often slightly glandular to the touch. Its leaves are shiny green above and paler on the underside. They are up to 4 inches long, oblong in outline and have sharply toothed margins. Leaves grow in an alternate pattern along the twig. Its winter buds are sharply pointed. Flowers are arranged in dense, cylindrical clusters called catkins. Male and female flowers are produced in separate catkins. Male catkins are elongate, pendulous and may be up to 4 inches long. Female catkins are about ½ inch long and cone-like. They are erect and develop on new summer twigs. The catkins bear many winged fruit, each enclosing a single nutlet.

Male Catkins

Habitat and Range: Sitka alder is abundant in Glacier's avalanche chutes and on steep mountain slopes. It also forms thickets in moist, open forest in the montane and subalpine zones. Its range extends south from Alaska, through western Canada, into the northwest portion of the United Sates.

Female Catkins

Notes: Mountain alder (*A. incana,* lower photo) also grows in Glacier National Park. It has rounded winter buds, develops catkins on twigs of the previous season and is more common at low elevations than Sitka alder. The Blackfeet Indians used a strong tea made from aged alder bark to treat tuberculosis. Other tribes used it to treat constipation and jaundice. Alder seeds are an important food for many songbirds, including pine siskins and goldfinches.

Mountain Alder

Bog Birch
Betula glandulosa
Birch Family (Betulaceae)

Description: Deciduous shrub growing 3–6 feet tall with erect, spreading branches. The twigs are covered with fine hair and bear distinctive wart-like resin blisters. Its leaves are round to oblong in outline, ½–1 inch long, and toothed along their margins. They are somewhat leathery to the touch. The leaves turn brilliant scarlet-brown in late fall. Flowers are arranged in dense clusters called catkins. Male and female flowers are produced in separate catkins. Male catkins are grouped in clusters of 1 to 4. They are elongate, tubular and pendulous. Female catkins are elliptical in outline, erect, and ½–1 inch long when mature. They bear tiny, hardened, winged seeds.

Habitat and Range: Bog birch is common in wet, organic soil of fens and marshes below the subalpine zone. In the Park it grows on both sides of the Continental Divide, but is more common on the west side. It grows throughout Alaska and Canada, and in the northwest portion of the United States.

Notes: Despite its common name, bog birch does not grow in bogs in the northern Rocky Mountains. Bogs receive moisture only through precipitation. There are no true bogs within Glacier National Park. The "boggy areas" are actually fens, which are fed from groundwater. Grouse feed on the catkins, buds and seeds of birches.

Willows 101

Figuring out which willow is which is a difficult task. Even the most experienced botanists struggle with willows because they all look so similar. This section is intended to provide the reader with enough basic knowledge of willow characteristics to identify at least a handful of the 23 species that grow in Glacier National Park.

Willows (*Salix* spp.) are members of the Willow Family (Salicaceae). In and around the Park willows are mostly shrubs, ranging in size from 3 inch, mat-forming plants to tall shrubs growing up to 10 feet. Two willow species, crack willow (pg. 72) and peachleaf willow (pg.74), are considered trees and discussed in the "Tree" section of this book. Since their growth form is so different they are easier to separate from the "shrubby" willow species.

Male Catkins - Crack Willow

Perhaps the most distinguishing feature of willows is the catkin, an elongated structure, composed of a cluster of 25 or more flowers. Catkins are borne on short, leafy twigs of the current year's growth or may be directly attached to previous year's twigs. Willow flowers are different than typical flowers because they lack petals and sepals. The only visible flower parts are the stamens (male flower parts) and pistils (female flower parts). Male and female flowers are produced on separate plants (dioecious), so some plants will have catkins composed of only male flowers while others will have only female catkins.

Female Catkins - Dusky Willow

Mature male catkins (upper photo) are a fluffy collection of thread-like filaments tipped with yellow anthers. Filaments and anthers are the two structures that make up a stamen. The male catkins of some willows are soft and fluffy, and referred to as "pussy willows." Mature female catkins are composed of many pistils that mature into firm, seed-bearing capsules (lower right photo). The capsules of separate willow species have different

Mix of Shrubby Willow Species Bordering a Wetland

characteristics, such as hair or a stalk at the base. These characteristics are very help-ful in correctly identifying a willow species.

The characteristics of willow leaves are another important component in identifying willows. But not just any leaves. Mature leaves are crucial for making an accurate determination. The leaves are densely hairy on some species and sparsely hairy on others. The leaves of one species may be long and slender, while those of another species may be lance-shaped. Another important character is whether or not leaves have a glaucous bloom (a whitish, waxy film) and are lighter in color on the leaf underside, compared with the upper surface.

A person who has spent any time at all trying to identify willow species will quickly discover the central problem with willows: mature catkins and mature leaves are not always available at the same time. While this discovery can indeed be frustrating, figuring out which willow is which is still very possible. Examining a range of plant characteristics will usually lead to either a correct answer or whittle the answer down to a few possibilities.

While the description of all 23 willow species is beyond the scope of this book, the photos and text in the following pages present the Park's most common willows. Details for each species include both catkin and leaf characters, and are intended to make their identification relatively straightforward. For more information on the Park's willows see Peter Lesica's Flora of Glacier National Park.

Arctic Willow
Salix arctica
Willow Family (Salicaceae)

Description: Deciduous, mat-forming shrub with trailing stems rarely growing more than 3 inches tall. Its leaves are narrowly elliptic in outline and ½–1½ inches long. They are shiny green on the upper surface. The lower surface is waxy-pale and often sparsely hairy. The leaf blade tapers toward the petiole (leaf stalk). Flowers are produced in elongated clusters of more than 25 on erect stalks (catkins), at the tips of leafy shoots. Male and  female flowers are produced on separate plants. Female catkins are most useful for identification. They are about ½–1¼ inches long. Flowers of female catkins mature into seed-bearing capsules, each about ¼ inch long and hairy. Arctic willow blooms in July and August.

Habitat and Range: Arctic willow is abundant on exposed alpine ridges and slopes, and in alpine meadows and turf. Mats often form along streams or where snow lies late into the summer. Its range extends from Alaska and British Columbia east to Greenland and Newfoundland. It occurs in all Canadian Provinces except for Saskatchewan. In the lower 48 states it occurs in Washington, Oregon, Idaho, Montana and Vermont.

Notes: Because it has such a low growth form, most observers don't think of arctic willow as a shrub. Since its trailing stems are woody it is indeed classified as a "dwarf shrub." Arctic willow often grows with snow willow (*S. reticulata*), another low-growing shrub. Snow willow has smaller catkins (less than ½ inch long), and its leaf blades are rounded where they meet the petiole. The Blackfeet Tribe had many medicinal uses for willows. A strong tea made from willow roots was used to remedy throat pain and internal bleeding. Arctic willow attracts large numbers of native bees, and is important for sustaining native bee populations.

Undergreen Willow
Salix commutata
Willow Family (Salicaceae)

Description: Deciduous shrub growing 1–5 feet high. Its twigs are dark and covered with long hair. Leaves are elliptic in outline and 1–3 inches long. They are sparsely long-hairy and pale green on both sides of the leaf. The leaf margins may be shallowly toothed or smooth. Male and female flowers are produced on separate plants, and are arranged into elongated clusters (catkins). Female catkins are the most helpful for plant identification. They are 1–2 inches long, composed of more than 25 flowers and produced on leafy stalks. Flowers mature into smooth, short-stalked capsules, less than ¼ inch long, with a tiny style projecting from the top. Undergreen willow blooms in July and August.

Habitat and Range: Undergreen willow is abundant near treeline in moist soil along streams, ponds and wetlands, especially in areas where snow accumulates. Its range extends from Alaska south, through British Columbia and Alberta, to Oregon, Idaho and Montana.

Notes: Undergreen willow lacks a "glaucous bloom" that is common among willows. A glaucus bloom is a thin, waxy coating. It is common on the underside of willow leaves, making the surface lighter in color, compared to the upper surface. Booth's willow (*S. boothii*, left lower photo) also lacks the glaucous bloom, like undergreen willow, but its leaves are smooth and hairless. It is common along streams, lakes and wetlands in the montane and subalpine zones. Grey-leaved willow (*S. glauca*, right lower photo) is another willow that is common in the upper subalpine zone. It grows in moist meadows and on limestone talus slopes. The leaves of grey-leaved willow have a glaucous bloom and are sparsely long-hairy on the underside.

Booth's Willow   **Grey-leaved Willow**

Drummond's Willow
Salix drummondiana
Willow Family (Salicaceae)

Description: Deciduous shrub with tall, spreading branches growing 3–10 feet high. Its young twigs are usually gray with a thin, waxy coating (glaucous bloom). Its leaves are narrowly elliptic to oblong in outline and 1–3 inches long. The upper leaf surface is green, while the underside is densely covered with silver hair at maturity. Male and female flowers are produced on separate plants, and are arranged into erect, elongated clusters (catkins). Female catkins are composed of more than 25 flowers and are 1–3 inches long. They are produced along the twigs of the previous year. The flowers mature into seed-bearing, hairy capsules, each less than ¼ inch long. Drummond's willow blooms from May to July.

Habitat and Range: Drummond's willow is abundant in the Park's montane and subalpine zones, along lakes, ponds, streams and wetlands. It also grows on rocky slopes and glacial moraine. Its range extends from northwestern Canada south to California and New Mexico.

Notes: The leaves of many willow species are hairy on the underside when young, but the hair usually falls off at maturity. It's important to obtain mature leaves, as well as catkins, to accurately identify willows. The felt-like underside of Drummond's willow leaves is intact even at maturity. The leaves of Sitka willow (*S. sitchensis,* left) and sageleaf willow (*S. candida*, right), also have hair on the underside at maturity. Sitka willow has short-hairy, waxless twigs. Sageleaf willow leaves are densely white-hairy on both surfaces, and plants usually occur in wet, peaty soil. Its young twigs are thickly covered with white hair. Drummond's willow is the most common of these three willows.

Sageleaf Willow   **Sitka Willow**

Dusky Willow
Salix melanopsis
Willow Family (Salicaceae)

Description: Deciduous shrub growing up
to 6½ feet tall with brown twigs. Its leaves
are 1½–3 inches long and linear to narrowly
elliptic in outline. They are usually at least
six times as long as they are wide. Leaves
are mostly hairless. They are green on the
upper surface and have a pale, waxy coating (glaucous bloom) on the underside. The
leaf margins are shallowly toothed. Male
and female flowers are produced on separate
plants, and are arranged into erect, elongated
clusters (catkins). Female catkins, produced
at the tips of leafy branchlets, are composed
of more than 25 flowers and are ¾–1½ inches long. Flowers mature into seed-bearing,
hairless capsules, each less that ¼ inch long.
They are attached to the center of the catkin
by a tiny stalk.

Habitat and Range: Dusky willow is common in the Park's montane and subalpine
zones, forming thickets along rivers, streams
and lakes. Its range extends from British
Columbia and Alberta south to California, Utah and Colorado.

Notes: Dusky willow is sometimes mistaken for
sandbar willow (*S. exigua*, left photo), a species
that occurs in the park but is less common. The two
species are closely related. The leaves of sandbar
willow are typically longer, narrower and lighter
green than those of dusky willow. Sandbar willow's
capsules are sometimes hairy, while the capsules of
dusky willow are smooth and hairless. Sandbar willow grows along mountain streams and on alluvial
bars in the montane zone. Native Americans used
the stems and branches of willows for arrow shafts,
paint brushes and baskets. Rabbits, deer, elk and
moose eat willow bark, twigs and foliage.

Sandbar Willow

Rock Willow
Salix vestita
Willow Family (Salicaceae)

Description: Deciduous, low shrub growing 8–40 inches tall. Its leaves are deep green and distinctly veined on the upper surface. The lower surface is covered with dense, white hair. Leaves are elliptic to ovate in outline with down-rolled margins. Male and female flowers are produced on separate plants, and are arranged into erect, elongated clusters (catkins). Female catkins are composed of more than 25 flowers and are ¾–1½ inches long. Flowers mature into seed-bearing, hairy capsules, each less that ¼ inch long. Rock willow blooms in July and August.

Habitat and Range: Rock willow is abundant on moist, rocky slopes, ledges and in wet meadows in the Park's alpine and subalpine zones. Its range includes British Columbia, Alberta, Washington, Oregon and Montana. Its range also includes much of eastern Canada, from Nunavut and Manitoba east to Newfoundland and Nova Scotia.

Notes: Rock willow is one of the easiest high-elevation willows to identify in Glacier National Park because its leaves are so unique. The deeply impressed veins on the leaf upper surface and very narrow female catkin are diagnostic characters which separate rock willow from all other alpine and subalpine willows.

Rocky Mountain Maple
Acer glabrum
Maple Family (Aceraceae)

Description: Rocky Mountain maple typically grows as a cluster of slender stems,
each up 20 feet high. Branches are usually
paired opposite each other. It is most often
described as a tall shrub. Occasionally it
will develop a single-trunk, tree-like growth
form. The bark of its trunk is gray and has
a rough texture. Twigs are red, smooth and
somewhat shiny. Its leaves have a typical
maple leaf shape, with 3 to 5 pointed lobes.
The leaf margin is double-toothed, with
coarse, larger teeth bearing smaller teeth
along the edge. Leaves are 1–5 inches wide

Leaves and Fruit

and borne opposite each other along twigs.
Separate male and female flowers are produced by
Rocky Mountain maple. Both are green, less than
½ inch in diameter and inconspicuous. Female
flowers mature into fruit composed of two fused
seeds, each with a large, thin wing. Each individual seed and wing structure is about ¾–1½ inch
long. Strong winds can carry the winged seeds
high into the air and great distances.

Flowers

Habitat and Range: Rocky Mountain maple occupies moist valley forests, open, rocky mountain
slopes and subalpine avalanche chutes. It grows
extensively across the western United States. It is
also common throughout British Columbia and in
southwestern Alberta. Its range extends north into the
Yukon Territories, near the Pacific Coast.

Notes: Tiny, red, bladder-like bumps on the surface
of Rocky Mountain maple leaves are galls formed
by infestations of gall mites (lower photo). The galls
start out green, turn red, then black. They start to

Gall Mites

form when mites feed on leaf tissue in early spring. As the mites feed and the leaf
continues to grow, leaf tissue grows out and around the mite, forming the tiny gall.
In autumn, Rocky Mountain maple casts brilliant shades of red and gold in the forest
understory. Native Americans had many uses for its sturdy wood, including snow-
shoes, bows and cradle frames. Medicinally, northwest tribes used a tea made from
the branches to heal skin lesions and reduce inflammation.

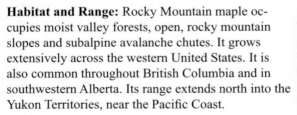

Devil's Club
Oplopanax horridus
Ginseng Family (Araliaceae)

Description: Deciduous shrub growing 3–7 feet tall with densely spiny stems. Its leaves are large (4–12 inches wide) with a distinct maple-leaf shape. The lower leaf surface is densely covered with spines along the veins. Numerous, greenish colored flowers are produced on an erect stalk, 3–8 inches long. Fruit are bright red berries, about ¼ inch long, borne in showy, pyramidal clusters. Devil's club blooms in June and July.

Habitat and Range: In Glacier National Park devil's club is commonly found in moist to wet montane forests on the west side of the Continental Divide, where it often grows in dense thickets. East of the Divide it occurs in deep, moist valleys. In the greater northwest, Devil's Club grows in southern Alaska, south through the Canadian provinces of British Columbia and Alberta, into Washington, northern Idaho, northwest Montana and western Oregon.

Notes: Native Americans used the inner stems to treat cold and flu symptoms. Early American settlers used root extracts to treat diabetes. The berries are poisonous and should not be ingested, but the early spring shoots and leaves are edible. The leaves become inedible once the leaf spines begin to stiffen.

Big Sagebrush
Artemisia tridentata
Sunflower Family (Asteraceae)

Description: Erect shrub with aromatic foliage growing 15–40 inches tall. Its leaves are narrow and densely covered with silvery hair. They are ½–1¼ inches long and wider at the tip than the base. The tip is shallowly divided into 3 lobes. Its tiny flowers are tightly clustered into disk-shaped heads, less than ¼ inch high. Many heads loosely arranged in tall, branched cluster at branch tips. Big sagebrush blooms in August and September.

Habitat and Range: Big sagebrush is common in open grasslands near the North Fork Flathead River, on the west side of Glacier National Park. It can also be found growing in dry, open areas throughout the western United States and Canada.

Notes: Big sagebrush provides habitat for many birds and animals. Mule deer and white-tailed deer browse the twigs and foliage. Brewer's sparrow, a songbird found only in sagebrush habitat, occurs in Glacier's sagebrush prairies. Native Americans across the northwest United States used big sagebrush extensively for its medicinal properties. A strong tea made from the leaves was used to alleviate stomach pain, pneumonia, and as a cure for the common cold. A poultice of the leaves was used to ease rheumatism pain and inflammation.

Alder-leaved Buckthorn
Rhamnus alnifolia
Buckthorn Family (Rhamnaceae)

Description: Deciduous shrub with erect, spreading branches growing 1–6 feet tall. Its twigs are covered with short hair. Its leaves are broadly lance-shaped in outline with 5 to 7 prominent veins extending from the leaf base toward the tip. The leaves are 1–5 inches long and arranged alternately along branches. Male and female flowers are produced on separate plants. They are short-stalked and arise in groups of 2 to 5 from the axils of lower leaves. Each flower is green, less than ¼ inch wide, and has 5 sepals and no petals. Fruits are berry-like drupes, each about ¼ inch long. They are initially green then turn black at maturity. Alder-leaved buckthorn blooms in May and June.

Habitat and Range: Alder-leaved buckthorn is abundant in wet forest openings, and along marshes, swamps, lakes and fens in the Park. In Canada it occurs from British Columbia to Newfoundland. Its range extends across the northern United States from Washington and Oregon to New England, and south to California, Wyoming, Ohio and Virginia.

Notes: Buckthorn bark was used by Native Americans to induce vomiting and as a laxative. Herbalists prescribe elixirs made from the bark to alleviate constipation. It is described as being somewhat harsh and fast acting, so must be used in moderation. Woodpeckers and a wide range of songbirds feed on the berries.

Utah Honeysuckle
Lonicera utahensis
Honeysuckle Family (Caprifoliaceae)

Description: Deciduous shrub
growing 3–6 feet tall with
branched, leafy stems. Its leaves
are oblong in outline and 1–3
inches long. They have entire
(smooth) margins, a blunt tip, and
are arranged opposite each other
along the twigs. Paired, cream-colored flowers grow from the joint
between leaf and stem (leaf axil).
Flowers are broadly tube-shaped
with a bulge at the base. Pairs of
bright red berries are produced in
late summer. They are each about
¼ inch wide and fused at the base.
Flowers and berries are often hidden underneath the leaves. Utah
honeysuckle blooms in June and
July.

Flowers

Habitat and Range: Utah honeysuckle
is common in moist sites with partial sun
and can often be found in open forest, on
stream banks and along trails. Its range
extends from the Canadian provinces of
British Columbia and Alberta, through
the northwestern US, to Arizona and New
Mexico.

Notes: The berries of Utah honeysuckle
are edible. They have a juicy texture and
pleasant flavor. Birds, bears and other
animals use them as a food source.

Fruit

Black Elderberry
Sambucus racemosa
Honeysuckle Family (Caprifoliaceae)

Description: Deciduous shrub growing up to 10 feet tall. The branches have a waxy coating, giving them a grayish cast. Its leaves are divided into 5 to 9 lance-shaped leaflets. Each leaflet is toothed along its margin, 2–6 inches long and tapers to a slender point. Flowers are cream-colored, less than ¼ inch wide and saucer-shaped. They are arranged in a pyramidal-shaped cluster at branch tips. Berries are shiny, black and just under ¼ inch in diameter. Black elderberry blooms in June and July.

Habitat and Range: Black elderberry is common in shrubby thickets, avalanche chutes and moist, open forest. It occurs in the montane and lower subalpine zones of Glacier National Park. It grows in similar habitats throughout western Canada and the western United States.

Notes: Blue elderberry (*S. caerulea,* right) occurs in open, low-elevation forests south of the Park. It has been recorded near the town of Saint Mary, just outside the Park boundary, where it was likely planted as an ornamental. Its fruit are blue, with a thin, waxy coating. Black and blue elderberries have been used to make wine and jam for centuries. Some people have experienced nausea from eating the raw berries; others eat them with no adverse affects. Several sources describe the raw berries as poisonous and cooked berries as edible. They are high in iron and have been used by herbalists to treat anemia. Elderberry washes have been used by Native Americans and modern-day herbalists to treat skin ulcers and eczema.

Blue Elderberry

Low-bush Cranberry
Viburnum edule
Honeysuckle Family (Caprifoliaceae)

Description: Deciduous shrub with spreading stems up to 6½ feet tall. Its leaves are maple-leaf shaped with 3 pointed lobes and toothed margins. They are 1–4 inches long. The leaf underside is sparsely covered with hair and tiny glands. Flat-topped clusters of white flowers are produced at stem tips. Each flower is shallowly conical below and deeply 5-lobed above. They are about ½ inch wide. Fruit are red to orange berries, each ¼–½ inch in diameter. They form a bright cluster at branch tips in the fall. Low-bush cranberry blooms in June and July.

Habitat and Range: In Glacier National Park low-bush cranberry occupies moist margins of streams and wetlands in the subalpine and montane zones, mainly west of the Continental Divide. Its range includes Alaska and Canada, extending south into the northern United States.

Notes: This plant is used by herbalists to treat intestinal cramps and muscle spasms, and is aptly called "cramp bark" by some people. Another popular common name is mooseberry. Although low-bush cranberries are not related to traditional cranberries, which are in the Heath Family, they can be made into a sauce with the addition of water, gelatin and sugar. The berries are an important food source for many songbirds, including robins, flycatchers and cedar waxwings.

Red Osier Dogwood
Cornus sericea
Dogwood Family (Cornaceae)

Description: Deciduous shrub growing 3–10 feet tall with dark red bark. Its leaves are oval in outline and 1–6 inches long with short hair on the leaf underside. Long, prominent veins run the length of the leaf, parallel to the leaf margin. Flowers are white, 4-petaled and less than ¼ inch in diameter. They are arranged in open, flat-topped clusters at the ends of branches. Berry-like fruit are white to bluish white and about ¼ inch wide. Red osier dogwood blooms from May to July.

Flowers

Habitat and Range: Red osier dogwood is abundant in moist, partially open sites such as avalanche chutes and stream banks. It is also common in moist to wet mountain forests. Its range extends from Alaska, eastward across all of Canada. It grows across the entire lower 48 states, with the exception of Texas, Oklahoma and the southeastern states.

Fruit

Notes: Our plants are *Cornus sericea* subspecies *stolonifera*. Some botanists call the plant *Cornus stolonifera*. Native Americans used the wood of this plant for arrows, digging sticks and other tools. They used the inner bark to treat liver problems and lung ailments. The roots were used to alleviate diarrhea and as a mild astringint. The berries are edible and were collected by Native Americans for use as food. Deer and a wide variety of songbirds also eat the berries.

Labrador Tea
Ledum glandulosum
Heath Family (Ericaceae)

Description: Evergreen shrub with erect branches growing 1–2 feet tall. Its twigs are hairy, reddish in color, and often dotted with tiny glands. Its leaves are oval to elliptic in outline and grow in an alternate pattern along the branches. They are leathery, ½–3 inches long and slightly rolled under along the margins. The upper leaf surface is shiny, while the lower surface is dotted with small resin glands. Its flowers are white, dish-shaped and clustered at branch tips. Each flower is roughly ½ inch wide and has 5 petals and 8 to 12 long, thread-like stamens. Its fruit is a tiny oval-shaped capsule. Labrador tea blooms in May and June.

Habitat and Range: Labrador tea is common in moist soil of swamps, thickets and spruce forest on the west side of the Continental Divide in the Park. It often forms a ring surrounding wetlands just upland from saturated soil. It is primarily confined to western North America. Its range extends from the Canadian provinces of British Columbia and Alberta south to California, Nevada and Utah.

Notes: Labrador tea, made from the dried leaves of this plant, has been used extensively to treat sore throat pain, lice, chiggers, and as a sedative. In large amounts, however, it can cause muscle cramps, dizziness, paralysis and even death.

Cascade Azalea
Rhododendron albiflorum
Heath Family (Ericaceae)

Description: Deciduous shrub with erect stems growing 3–7 feet tall. Its leaves and twigs are covered with reddish hairs. The leaves are deep green on the upper surface and lighter beneath. They are elliptic in outline and 2–4 inches long. Flowers are born in clusters of 1 to 4 along the stems. Each flower is composed of 5 petals, fused at the base, forming a shallow, bell-like corolla. Ten stamens protrude from inside the petals and surround a central ovary. Stamens and ovary are densely hairy. Fruits are short, thick-walled capsules. Cascade azalea blooms from June to August.

Habitat and Range: Cascade azalea occupies moist sites in the montane zone. It is common along streams. It has not been documented in Glacier National Park but does occur south of the Park in the Bob Marshall Wilderness Area. In Waterton Lakes National Park it has been recorded near Glacier Park's western boundary, near Twin Lakes and Lost Lake. Its Canadian range includes British Columbia and Alberta. In the United States it occurs in Washington, Oregon, Idaho and Montana. It has also been documented in northern Colorado.

Notes: This plant is also known as white rhododendron. Several native North American tribes used various parts of this plant as medicine. A poultice was made from burned Cascade azalea wood and applied to burns and cuts to reduce pain and swelling. A strong tea made from the buds was used to treat colds and sore throats.

Sticky Currant
Ribes viscosissimum
Gooseberry Family (Grossulariaceae)

Description: Deciduous shrub with ascending branches growing 20–40 inches tall. Its branches lack barbs and bristles. Its leaves are divided into 3 to 5 palmate lobes, 1–4 inches wide and covered with soft, glandular hair, making them slightly sticky to the touch. Its flowers are white, bell-shaped and produced in clusters of 3 to 7 along

branches. They are ½–¾ inch long and sometimes tinged with pink. Black berries, just under ½ inch long, are produced in late summer. The berries are covered with gland tipped hair, giving them a slightly sticky texture. Sticky currant blooms from May to July.

Habitat and Range: Sticky currant is common in avalanche chutes, shrublands and moist to dry forests in the Park's montane and subalpine zones. Its range extends from British Columbia and Alberta south to California and Arizona.

Notes: Stinking currant (*R. hudsonianum*, right) also grows in the Park. It also lacks thorns and bristles, like sticky currant. Stinking currant produces many flowers in a spike-like cluster, instead of several flowers in a hemispheric cluster like sticky currant. The berries of stinking currant are covered with glands, but lack the gland-tipped hair that is present on sticky currant berries.

Stinking Currant

Mock Orange
Philadelphus lewisii
Hydrangea Family (Hydrangeaceae)

Description: Deciduous shrub with erect, spreading branches up to 9 feet tall. Its twigs are reddish brown and smooth. Its leaves are broadly lance-shaped and 1–2½ inches long. The leaf margins are entire (smooth) and there are 3 prominent veins running from the leaf base toward the tip. Leaves are produced opposite each other along the branches. Its flowers are white with yellow centers and sweetly fragrant. Each flower has 4 petals and is about 1¼ inch wide. Its fruit are tiny, 4-chambered capsules, each ¼–½ inch long. Mock orange typically blooms in July.

Habitat and Range: Mock orange is common on dry, rocky slopes in the Park's montane zone, on both sides of the Continental Divide. It also occurs in moist shrublands along streams and rivers, and in avalanche chutes. Its range extends from British Columbia and Alberta south through Washington, Idaho, Montana, Oregon and central California.

Notes: Mock orange is the State Flower of Idaho, where it is commonly called syringa. It's sweet-smelling, 4-petaled blossoms are one of its most distinguishing characters. Mock orange has been used extensively by both Native Americans and modern-day herbalists. Ointments prepared from its branches have been used to treat inflammation, skin lesions and hemorrhoids. It makes a great ornamental in native landscaping.

Buckbrush
Ceanothus velutinus
Buckthorn Family (Rhamnaceae)

Description: Evergreen shrub with erect, spreading branches typically growing 2–4 feet tall. Plants may occasionally reach 5–6 feet. Its young twigs are green, and foliage is fragrant. Its leaves are oval in outline, shiny above, hairy below, and 1–3 inches long. Three prominent veins run from the base toward the tip. The leaves are arranged alternately along branches. Tiny, white, star-shaped flowers are produced in dense clusters at the tips of lower branches. Each flower is less than ¼ inch wide and has 5 hood-shaped petals. Its fruit are glandular-sticky, 3-lobed capsules. Each lobe has a low ridge along its back. Buckbrush blooms in June and July.

Habitat and Range: Buckbrush is common in relatively open forests, recently burned areas and along roads and trails from montane to subalpine. Its range extends from British Columbia and Alberta south to California, and east to South Dakota.

Notes: This plant is also known as show brush. Its dried leaves have been used as a substitute for tobacco and black tea. Herbalists have used it to relieve painful inflammation in many different areas of the body, including the throat, lymph nodes and adenoids. A strong tea made from the leaves has proven useful in reducing anxiety and internal bleeding. Buckbrush readily colonizes burned areas because its seeds depend on fire for germination. Deer, elk and rabbits browse the twigs and foliage.

Serviceberry
Amelanchier alnifolia
Rose Family (Rosaceae)

Description: Deciduous shrub with several erect stems per plant growing up to 13 feet tall. Its leaves are broadly oval-shaped in outline and ¾–2 inches long. They are toothed along the upper portion of the leaf margin. Its flowers are white with 5 narrow, spatula-shaped petals, each about ½ inch long. Clusters of flowers are produced at branch tips. Fruits are fleshy, purple, berry-like pomes ¼–½ inch wide. Serviceberry blooms from April through July.

Habitat and Range: Serviceberry is abundant in moist to dry forests of the Park, where it has a tall and open growth form. It is also plentiful in Glacier's shrublands and grasslands where it is shorter and more compact. It often forms low thickets in disturbed soil of montane grasslands. Its range extends from Alaska east through Canada to New Brunswick and south to California, Colorado and Iowa.

Notes: Serviceberry is one of Glacier's most common shrubs. It is also known as saskatoon and juneberry. Serviceberries provide an important staple in the diets of bears and birds in the Park. The berries are edible, but some find them mealy, full of seeds and a bit tasteless. They were a frequent ingredient in Native American pemmican, a dried cake made of meat and fruit. Early American settlers used them extensively in preserves, pies and sauces. Serviceberry plants that grow in the sun generally produce more fruit than those in the shade.

Flower

Fruit

Black Hawthorn
Crataegus douglasii
Rose Family (Rosaceae)

Description: Deciduous shrub growing up to 13 feet tall, sometimes appearing like a small tree. Its branches bear large, straight thorns ½–1 inch long. Its leaves are elliptic in outline and 1–2½ inches long. They are shallowly lobed and toothed along the margin, especially toward the tip. White, 5-petaled flowers are produced in clusters at branch tips. Each flower is about ½ inch wide and bowl-shaped. Burgundy-colored, smooth, berry-like pomes form in summer, each about ½ inch in diameter. They turn blackish by early fall. Hawthorn blooms in June and July.

Full Shrub

Habitat and Range: Black hawthorn is common along streams, marshes and grasslands, and in open forests and shrublands of the Park. Its range extends from Washington and Oregon east to Michigan and south to California. It also occurs in Alaska, and across Canada in all provinces except Manitoba and New Brunswick.

Flowers

Notes: Black hawthorn is the only tall shrub in Glacier with long, straight, sharp thorns. A related species, Columbia hawthorn (*C. columbiana*), with red fruit and longer thorns, grows just southwest of the Park. Hawthorn berries provide food for birds, bears and other wildlife. The berries are frequently used in jams. Herbalists use the fruit and flowers to treat many ailments including anxiety and arteriosclerosis.

Fruit

Oce

Holo

Rose

Description: Deciduous
shrub growing 3–10 feet tall
with erect, arching branches.
Its leaves are ovate in outline
with shallowly toothed and
lobed margins. They are
1½–2½ inches long and
hairy, bright green above
and lighter-colored beneath.
Dense clusters of tiny, white,
saucer-shaped flowers are
produced at branch tips in a
pyramidal-shaped inflorescence. Each flower is about ¼
inch wide. Fruit are seed-like
achenes. They are small, hairy
and 1-seeded. Ocean spray
blooms in July and August.

Habitat and Range: Ocean
spray is common in open forests and shrublands that occupy the Park's montane zone.
It is especially common west
of the Continental Divide. Its
range extends from British
Columbia south to California and Arizona, and east to Colorado and Montana.

Notes: A strong tea made of ocean spray bark has been used by herbalists to relieve
stomach pain and diarrhea. It is also reported to stop bleeding and enhance internal
cleansing by stimulating the flow of urine. The strong bark has been used by many
Native American tribes for tools, bows and arrows.

Ninebark

Physocarpus malvaceus
Rose Family (Rosaceae)

Description: Deciduous shrub growing 3–7 feet tall with erect, arching branches and striped, gray and brown bark. Its leaves are ovate in outline and 1–3 inches long. They have 3 distinct lobes and toothed margins, resembling maple leaves, and are sparsely covered with star-shaped hairs. White, saucer-shaped flowers, about ½ inch long, are grouped in rounded clusters on branch tips. Each flower has a central cup-like disc called a hypanthium. Its fruit are fuzzy, brittle capsules, each about ¼ inch long. Ninebark blooms from May to July.

Habitat and Range: Ninebark is common on sunny, exposed slopes in the Park, especially near West Glacier and along the Middle Fork Flathead River. It often grows in the understory of open Douglas fir forests. Its range stretches from British Columbia and Alberta south to Nevada, Utah and Colorado.

Notes: Ninebark is frequently used in native plant gardens throughout the northwest United States. The roots were cooked and eaten by the Okanagan-Colville Indians of Washington and British Columbia. Members of this tribe also used the plant as a malicious charm, to put a spell of "bad luck" on others.

Bitter Cherry
Prunus emarginata
Rose Family (Rosaceae)

Description: Deciduous shrub or small tree growing 6–13 feet with purplish twigs. Its leaves are oblong in outline, toothed along the margins and rounded at the tip. The leaf blade is 1–3 inches long. There are 2 to 3 small, swollen glands on the leaf stalk (petiole) just below the leaf blade. Its flowers are white, cup-shaped and borne in a hemispheric cluster near the tips of branches. The cluster is composed of 5 to 8 flowers, each about ½ inch wide. Twenty to 30 long, thread-like stamens protrude from the flower center. Fruits are red to black, 1-seeded, cherry-like drupes, ¼–½ inch in diameter.

Habitat and Range: Bitter cherry is common in open forest, shrubby thickets, avalanche chutes and along streams in Glacier's montane and lower subalpine zones. In the Park it occurs on the west side of the Continental Divide. Its range stretches from British Columbia south to California, Arizona and New Mexico.

Notes: A similar species, pin cherry (*P. pensylvanica*) also grows in Glacier National Park, but is much less common. In the Park it occurs on the east side of the Continental Divide. Its leaves taper to a point, instead of rounding at the tip like the leaves of bitter cherry. Look for pin cherry east of the Continental Divide in the Cut Bank and Two Medicine valleys. Pin cherry's range extends across Canada, from British Columbia to Newfoundland. In the United States it mainly grows east of the Continental Divide from Montana to New England, and south to Wyoming, Illinois and North Carolina.

Chokecherry
Prunus virginiana
Rose Family (Rosaceae)

Description: Deciduous shrub or small tree growing up to 17 feet tall with purplish gray bark. Twigs have scattered lenticels Its leaves are elliptic in outline with a pointed tip and toothed along the margins. They are 1½–4 inches long and bear 2 to 3 distinctly swollen glands on the leaf stalk (petiole) just below the leaf blade. Its flowers are saucer-shaped, 5-petaled and about ½ inch wide. They are produced in cylindrical clusters at branch tips. Fruit are small cherries, about ½ inch in diameter. They are red when first produced, becoming dark with age, and hang downward in long clusters. Chokecherry blooms from May to July.

Flowers

Habitat and Range: Chokecherry is common in the Park in shrubby thickets that border streams and grasslands. It also frequently occurs in forest openings and avalanche chutes. It occurs in Alaska and Canada from British Columbia to Manitoba. In the lower 48 United States chokecherry's range extends from Washington south to California, and east to the Dakotas, Nebraska and Kansas.

Notes: Glacier's chokecherry plants are variety *melanocarpa*. The flesh of chokecherry fruit is edible, but the pit contains a toxic substance (hydrocyanic acid) that is potentially fatal if ingested in large amounts. Chokecherries have been used in jam, wine and syrup for centuries. Native Americans relied on the fruit as an addition to pemmican, an important winter provision made of meat and fruit. They used a tea made from the inner bark to treat a variety of ailments, including headache and heart trouble. Chockecherries are an important food for bears, becoming critical in years when the huckleberry crop is sparse.

Fruit

Wild Red Raspberry
Rubus idaeus
Rose Family (Rosaceae)

Description: Deciduous shrub with prickly stems growing up to 5 feet tall. Its leaves are palmately divided into 3 to 5 toothed, lance-shaped leaflets, each 1–3 inches long. Clusters of 1 to 4 white flowers are produced from the axils of upper leaves (where the leaf meets the branch). They are about ½ inch wide with 5 slender petals and 5 glandular, reflexed, leaf-like sepals. Wild red raspberry blooms in June and July.

Flower

Fruit

Habitat and Range: Wild red raspberry is common on rocky stream banks, rock slides and burned slopes in the Park's montane and lower subalpine zones, on both sides of the Continental Divide. It occurs throughout most of North America, from Alaska and northern Canada south to California, New Mexico and North Carolina.

Notes: Black raspberry (*R. leucodermis*), also occurs in Glacier National Park, on the west side of the Continental Divide, but is uncommon. It has hooked spines along its branches. All wild raspberries are edible. They are great trail food, and were used extensively by Native Americans and early settlers. The flowers are also edible. An infusion of the leaves has been used by herbalists to eliminate nausea in pregnancy and reduce labor pains during delivery. Spiny-armed plants, such as raspberries, provide important cover for birds and small mammals.

Thimbleberry
Rubus parviflorus
Rose Family (Rosaceae)

Description: Deciduous shrub growing up to 5 feet tall with shredding, peeling bark. Its branches are unarmed, and leaves are palmately divided, like maple leaves, into 3 to 7 pointed lobes. The leaves are 2–6 inches wide and bristly-hairy on both surfaces. Open clusters of white, 5-petaled flowers are produced on stem tips. Flowers are saucer-shaped and 1–2 inches wide. Fruits are produced in hemispheric clusters, somewhat like raspberries. They are small, juicy and single-seeded. Thimbleberry blooms in June and July.

Habitat and Range: Thimbleberry is abundant along trails in the montane and subalpine zones of Glacier National Park, where it grows in moist forests, shrublands and avalanche chutes. In Canada thimbleberry occurs in British Columbia, Alberta and Ontario. In the United States its range includes Alaska and most western states. It also occurs in the north-central U.S. from South Dakota to Michigan.

Notes: Thimbleberries are edible. They are juicy and sweet, and have been used as food by native residents for centuries. The berries were used internally by the Black-feet Tribe to alleviate chest ailments. Other tribes made a strong tea of the leaves to heal digestive trouble. A poultice of the leaves was applied to wounds to promote healing. The berries are also extensively used by a wide variety of songbirds, including chickadees and cedar waxwings.

Western Mountain Ash
Sorbus scopulina
Rose Family (Rosaceae)

Description: Deciduous shrub with tall, spreading branches up to 10 feet tall. Its twigs are covered with fine, short, white hair. Its leaves are pinnately divided into 9 to 13 narrowly lance-shaped, toothed leaflets. Each leaflet is 1–3 inches long and pointed at the tip. Its tiny, white flowers are produced in a dense, flat-topped cluster of 70 to 200. Fruits are initially orange, becoming red over time. They are berry-like, about ¼ inch in diameter, and tightly clustered at branch tips. Western mountain ash blooms in June and July.

Flowers

Fruit

Habitat and Range: Western mountain ash is common where there is deep winter snow. It occurs in the Park's moist subalpine forests, shrubby slopes and avalanche chutes. It also occurs in the montane zone but is less common.

Notes: A related species, Sitka mountain ash (*S. sitchensis*), also grows in Glacier National Park but is less common. Its twigs are red-hairy and its leaflets are rounded at the tip. Almost all parts of mountain ash plants have been used medicinally. The cooked berries are reported to alleviate throat inflammation. A strong tea made from the bark eases throat pain. All parts of the plant are described as having "astringent properties," which are useful for stopping hemorrhage and diarrhea. Mountain ash berries persist through the winter, making them especially important as food for wildlife. Many birds, including cedar waxwings, grosbeaks and grouse, regularly feed on the berries.

Birch-leaved Spiraea
Spiraea betulifolia
Rose Family (Rosaceae)

Description: Deciduous shrub
with stems 8–32 inches tall sprouting from spreading rhizomes. Its
leaves are oval in outline, toothed
toward the tip and 1–3½ inches
long. Each cup-shaped, white
flower is just under ¼ inch wide
with 5 petals and 25 to 50 long
stamens. The flowers are densely
grouped into flat-topped clusters,
1–3 inches wide. In fruit a cluster
of 5 capsules are produced. Each
capsule is less than ¼ inch long
and covered with short hair. Birch-
leaved spiraea blooms in July and
August.

Habitat and Range: Birch-leaved
spiraea is abundant in the understory of moist to dry forests, on
shrubby slopes, bordering grasslands and in avalanche chutes
throughout the Park. In Canada
it occurs in British Columbia and
Alberta. In the United States its range extends from Washington and Oregon to Minnesota.

Notes: Birch-leaved spiraea is one of the Park's most abundant shrubs. Our plants
are var. *lucida*. Flowering plants occur more often in sunny habitats than in the
shade. Herbalists use a strong tea made from the leaves and stem to treat stomach
pain. The common cold has been treated with a tea made of boiled stem.

Oregon Grape
Berberis repens
Barberry Family (Berberidaceae)

Description: Low growing and creeping with stems
2–12 inches long. Leaves are
arranged alternately along
the stem and are divided into
5 to 7 spiny-toothed leaflets,
similar to common holly
leaves. They are green above
(sometimes tinged with red
or purple) and dull green with
a whitish, powdery coating
(bloom) below. They persist
for two growing seasons, at
the end of which they turn
crimson and whither. Yellow,
globe-shaped flowers are
arranged in elongated
clusters at branch tips.
Each flower is less than
¼ inch long. Fruit are
waxy, bluish purple
berries. Oregon grape
blooms in May and June.

Flowers

Habitat and Range: In
Glacier National Park
Oregon grape grows
in montane forests
and shrublands, and in
subalpine forests to a
lesser extent. Its range
extends from British
Columbia and Alberta
south, throughout the western
United States.

Fruit

Notes: Mule deer and white-tailed deer eat the fruit of Oregon grape. The Blackfeet
used the bark and roots to treat kidney and stomach problems, and to relieve itch-
ing. Modern-day herbalists use Oregon grape to treat a wide variety of ailments. It is
used as a remedy for anemia and general malnutrition, and as a stimulant and mild
laxative. Oregon grape berries are edible and may be used in jam, jelly and wine.
Eating too many berries, however, has been reported to cause vomiting and diarrhea.

Bracted Honeysuckle
Lonicera involucrata
Honeysuckle Family (Caprifoliaceae)

Description: Deciduous shrub, 3–10 feet tall, with erect stems and branches. Its twigs are 4-sided. Leaves are oval in outline and 2–6 inches long. They are pointed at the tip and often broadest above the middle. The leaf underside is sparsely hairy and dotted with tiny glands. Flowers are tubular and pale yellow, hanging in pairs from the joint between leaf and stem (leaf axils). They are about ½ inch long and subtended by 2 large purple bracts. These bracts bend backward when the plant is in fruit. Fruit are shiny, glandular, black berries just under ½ inch in diameter. Bracted honeysuckle blooms in June and July.

Flowers

Habitat and Range: Bracted honeysuckle is common in Glacier's moist mountain forests, along streams and in avalanche chutes. It grows in similar habitats throughout Canada and the western US.

Notes: Bracted honeysuckle berries are an important food source for bears, birds and other animals. They are considered inedible to humans due to their bitter flavor, and are reported as poisonous by some sources. Some Native Americans used the berries to induce vomiting after poisoning.

Fruit

Silverberry
Elaeagnus commutata
Oleaster Family (Elaeagnaceae)

Description: Deciduous shrub growing up to 13 feet tall with spreading rhizomes. Its leaves are oval in outline, 1–3 inches long, and arranged in an alternate pattern along the stem. The upper leaf surface is silvery, while the underside is covered with rust-colored scales. The flowers are light yellow, funnel-shaped and about ½ inch long. They grow from leaf axils singly or in groups of 2 or 3. Fruits are silvery, berry-like and about ½ inch long, produced in the fall. Silverberry blooms in June and July.

Flowers

Fruit

Habitat and Range: Silverberry often forms thickets in well-drained rocky soil at lower elevations in the Park. It is common on gravel bars and floodplains, and along streams. Its range extends east from Alaska across Canada and south to Utah and Colorado. Isolated populations also have been recorded in Texas and Kentucky.

Notes: Silverberry gives off a distinctive, sweet aroma when blooming, much like Russian olive (pg. 64). The berries are edible but most people consider them mealy and unpalatable. Despite this fact, many Native American tribes gathered them for use as food. They mixed them with other substances, such as fat or sweeter berries, to improve their taste and texture. Some people call this shrub "wolf willow," although it is not a true willow.

Canada Buffaloberry
Shepherdia canadensis
Oleaster Family (Elaeagnaceae)

Description: Deciduous shrub with erect, spreading branches up to 10 feet high. Its twigs are covered with rust-colored scales when young. Its leaves are oval in outline, 1–3 inches long and arranged opposite each other along branches. They are dark green and shiny above and fuzzy beneath with rust-colored scales. Tiny, yellow flowers are clustered in the axils of new leaves. Clusters of bright reddish orange berries are produced in late summer. Flowers and berries are often hidden under leaves. Canada buffaloberry blooms in May and June.

Flowers

Habitat and Range: In the Park Canada buffaloberry occupies open forests and shrublands in the montane and lower subalpine zones. It also occurs in upper-elevation grasslands. Its range extends east from Alaska across Canada, and south through the western states of California, Arizona and New Mexico. In the eastern United States its range extends south as far as Illinois, Indiana and Ohio.

Notes: Canada buffaloberries are edible, but most people find them unpalatable. As with most berries, cooking them with added sugar dramatically improves their flavor. Native Americans mixed the berries with buffalo meat to make pemmican. Dried berries were also added to stews and puddings. Tribes also used the berries medicinally to alleviate stomach problems and constipation.

Fruit

Shrubby Cinquefoil
Pentaphylloides fruticosa
Rose Family (Rosaceae)

Description: Erect, spreading shrub growing 4–40 inches tall. Its leaves are pinnately divided into 5 narrowly lance-shaped leaflets, each about ½ inch long. They are sparsely covered with silky hair. Yellow, 5-petaled flowers are clustered in groups of 1 to 5. They arise from upper leaf axils. Its fruits are silky-hairy seed-like achenes, each about ½ inch long. Shrubby cinquefoil blooms from June to August.

Habitat and Range: Shrubby cinquefoil grows in a wide range of open habitats, at all elevations in the Park. It is common in mountain meadows and on subalpine and alpine slopes. Its range extends from Alaska south to California, Arizona and New Mexico, and east to Newfoundland, Massachusetts and New Jersey.

Flowers

Notes: This plant is also known by the scientific names *Potentilla fruitcosa* and *Dasiphora fruticosa*. It is an incredibly adaptable plant, able to flourish in almost any habitat. It is used extensively in gardens across the northern United States. Some garden cultivars have white flowers. A strong tea made from the leaves and flowers has been used to treat stomach pain, internal bleeding and inflammation of the esophagus. Chipmunks feed on the seeds and foliage of cinquefoils.

Common Snowberry
Symphoricarpos albus
Honeysuckle Family (Caprifoliaceae)

Description: Deciduous shrub growing up to 3 feet tall from spreading
rootstalks. Twigs are smooth and
hairless. Its leaves are oval in outline and 1–2 inches long, with entire
(not toothed) margins. They are
produced opposite each other along
twigs. Leaves on young twigs may
be shallowly lobed. Clusters of light
pink flowers are produced at the ends
of branches, and in some leaf axils.
The flower petals are fused into a
bell-shaped tube about ¼ inch long.
Ivory-colored berries, ¼–½ inch wide,
form in mid- to late-summer. Blooms
from June to August.

Flowers

Habitat and Range: Common
snowberry is abundant in moist
to dry, montane and subalpine
forests in the Park. It also grows
in Alaska, British Columbia,
and across much of the northern
United States, in similar habitats.

Notes: Our common snowberry
plants are var. *laevigatus*. Western snowberry (*S. occidentalis*,
inset photo) also grows in the

Fruit

Park, in more open habitat. It looks very similar to common snowberry, but its flower
petals are fused into a bowl-shaped corolla, and its young twigs are covered with
fine hair. These two snowberries are the only shrubs
in Glacier that produce large, ivory-colored berries.
The berries are considered mildly poisonous but can
be extremely toxic if consumed in large quantities,
especially by children. Grouse and chipmunks are the
only reported wildlife species that feed on the berries.
A poultice of the fresh leaves, fruit or bark has been
used by herbalists to treat cuts, sores and other skin
lesions.

Mountain Lover
Paxistima myrsinites
Bittersweet Family (Celastraceae)

Description: Evergreen shrub growing 8–30 inches tall with 4-sided, spreading branches. Its leaves are shiny-green and leathery with sharply toothed margins. They are ½–1 inch long and arranged opposite each other along twigs. Flowers are inconspicuous, dark reddish, 4-petaled and less than ¼ inch wide. They are produced in the joints between leaf and stem (leaf axils). Clusters of flowers are sometimes produced at branch tips. Fruit is a white, fleshy, oval capsule embedded in the central portion of the flower. Mountain lover blooms in May and June.

Habitat and Range: In the Park mountain lover is common in mountain forests and shrublands in the montane and subalpine zones. Its range extends from the Canadian provinces of British Columbia and Alberta, south through the western United States to Arizona and New Mexico.

Notes: Mountain lover is also known by the common names "mountain box" and "mountain boxwood." A strong tea made from mountain lover branches has been used by Native Americans to treat kidney trouble, tuberculosis and cold symptoms. A poultice of boiled leaves was applied to alleviate general pain and inflammation. This plant only occurs where it is sure to be snow-covered all winter.

Kinnikinnick
Arctostaphylos uva-ursi
Heath Family (Ericaceae)

Description: Low-growing and trailing evergreen shrub with branches reaching up to 6 inches tall. Its stems are covered with fine hair and slightly sticky to the touch. The leaves are oblong in outline, shiny and ½–1 inch long. They have a leathery texture. Pink flowers hang in clusters from branch tips. They are urn-shaped and less than ¼ inch long. Green berries are produced in the summer, turning red in the fall. They are ¼–½ inch wide. Kinnikinnick blooms in May and June.

Leaves and Flowers

Habitat and Range: Kinnikinnick is abundant in somewhat dry forests at all elevations in the Park. It is particularly common in the understory of conifer forests. It is also common in shrublands, grasslands, and in stony soil above treeline. Kinnikinnick grows in Alaska, eastward across Canada into Greenland, and southward to the western United States of California, Arizona and New Mexico. In the eastern US its southern range extends to Illinois, Indiana and Ohio.

Notes: Kinnikinnick is a popular food source for both black and grizzly bears, which is reflected in its scientific name. The Greek words *Arcto* and *staphylos* mean "a bear" and "a bunch of grapes" respectively. *Uva-ursi* is Latin for "bear's berries." Some people call the plant "bearberry."

Fruit

The berries are okay for human consumption but most people find them mealy and tasteless. The leaves were dried, mixed with tobacco and smoked by Native Americans. Herbalists have used the dried leaves in a tea to treat bronchitis, back pain and urinary tract problems.

Fool's Huckleberry
Menziesia ferruginea
Heath Family (Ericaceae)

Description: Deciduous shrub with arching branches and shredding bark, growing up to 7 feet tall. Its leaves are narrowly elliptic in outline and ¾–2½ inch long. They are finely toothed along the margin and broadest toward the tip, slightly hairy and sticky. The foliage gives off a distinctive skunk-like smell when crushed. Its flowers are pink- to orange-colored and urn-shaped. They are produced in clusters at the base of new twigs. Its fruit are firm capsules less than ½ inch in diameter. Fool's huckleberry blooms from June to August.

Habitat and Range: In the Park fool's huckleberry is abundant in the understory of forests in the montane and subalpine zones, especially under subalpine fir on north-facing slopes. Its range includes southern Alaska and the Canadian provinces of British Columbia and Alberta. It also occurs in the northwest portion of the lower 48 states, and in California.

Notes: True to its name, this plant is sometimes mistaken for common huckleberry (pg. 123). Fool's huckleberry is typically much taller with thinner, slightly sticky leaves, and it produces stiff capsules instead of edible berries like common huckleberry. Fool's huckleberry foliage contains poisonous alkaloids that can cause dizziness, weakness, headaches and paralysis. Early symptoms of poisoning are excessive salivation and vomiting. It can form impenetrable thickets on cool, moist slopes. Fool's huckleberry is sometimes called false azalea.

Dwarf Huckleberry
Vaccinium caespitosum
Heath Family (Ericaceae)

Description: Deciduous shrub up to 12 inches tall with spreading stems growing from rhizomes. Its leaves are ½–1½ inches long, oblong in outline and finely toothed along the margin. Its flower petals are fused into an urn-shaped corolla, about ¼ inch long. Flowers are pinkish and produced at the junction between leaf and stem (leaf axil). Its fruit are blue, waxy berries, just over ¼ inch wide. Dwarf huckleberry blooms in May and June.

Habitat and Range: Dwarf huckleberry is common in the Park's open montane and subalpine forests, especially spruce forests along rivers and streams. It is also common bordering grasslands and high-elevation meadows. Its range extends eastward from Alaska across Canada and south to California, New Mexico. In the western United States it occurs from Minnesota eastward to Maine.

Notes: This species is also known as dwarf billberry. Dwarf huckleberries, like all huckleberries (*Vaccinium* spp.), are edible. They are not as big and sweet as the more popular common huckleberry (facing page) and only rarely produce fruit compared to the other species. Huckleberries were used extensively by Native Americans for food and medicine. Both Natives and modern herbalists use this plant to cleanse the bladder and kidneys. A strong tea made from the bark has been used to alleviate cold symptoms.

Common Huckleberry
Vaccinium membranaceum
Heath Family (Ericaceae)

Description: Deciduous shrub, sometimes forming dense thickets, growing 1–3 feet high. Its leaves are broadly lance-shaped in outline, 1–2 inches long and finely toothed along their margins. Pink (sometimes yellowish green) flowers, about ¼ inch long and urn-shaped, are produced singly on stalks from the junction between leaf and stem (leaf axils). Its berries are initially red, turning deep purple at maturity. They are ¼–½ inch in diameter. Common huckleberry blooms in May and June; berries ripen from late July through August, depending on elevation and microclimate.

Flower

Habitat and Range: Common huckleberry is abundant in the understory of moist to dry forests in the montane and subalpine zones of the Park. It often forms open shrublands on slopes near treeline and where the overstory has been removed by fire. Beargrass (*Xerophyllum tenax*) frequently occurs with common huckleberry. Its range extends throughout western Canada and the United States, with the exception of Nevada, eastward to Michigan.

Berries

Notes: A similar huckleberry, globe huckleberry (*V. globulare*), is recognized as a separate species by some botanists. In the Park, however, the characters that separate common and globe huckleberry come together and the two species are indistinguishable. Huckleberries are Glacier's most well known berry. They are sweet, juicy and plentiful along most mountain trails. They can be used in jam and pies, and make a perfect trail snack. Park rules protect against over-picking, so check with Park staff for current huckleberry picking regulations. Huckleberries are also popular with Glacier's wildlife, particularly bears, who feed heavily on them in preparation for winter. Many birds, including grouse, thrushes and tanangers, rely on the fruit for summer and early fall foods.

Low Huckleberry
Vaccinium myrtillus
Heath Family (Ericaceae)

Description: Low-growing deciduous shrub up to 12 inches tall with distinctly angled twigs. The twigs are sparsely covered with short hair. Its leaves are about an inch long, lance-shaped and finely toothed along the margin. Flowers are pinkish, urn-shaped and about ¼ inch long. They are produced in leaf axils along the branches. Its berries are initially green and firm, gradually turning red, then dark blue at maturity. Low huckleberry typically blooms in June.

Habitat and Range: Low huckleberry is abundant in the understory of montane and subalpine forests, especially those dominated by lodgepole pine, subalpine fir and/ or spruce. Its range extends from British Columbia and Alberta south to Arizona and New Mexico. It also occurs in Greenland.

Notes: This species is Glacier's most common low-growing huckleberry. It closely resembles grouse whortleberry (facing page). The berries it produces are sweet and delicious, but much smaller than those produced by common huckleberry (previous page). Velvet-leaf huckleberry (*V. myrtilloides*, inset photo) is a taller huckleberry species that also grows in the Park. Its leaves have velvety hair on the veins, midribs and along the leaf margins. It is only known in Montana from several locations around West Glacier and Apgar, where it is locally abundant along the bike trail between Apgar and the West Entrance Station.

Velvet-leaf Huckleberry

Grouse Whortleberry
Vaccinium scoparium
Heath Family (Ericaceae)

Description: Deciduous shrub with erect, angled branches growing up to 8 inches tall. Its leaves are oval in outline, ¼–¾ inches long and finely toothed along the margins. Tiny, pinkish white flowers, less than ¼ inch long, grow singly from leaf axils. Fruit are a tiny, bright red to reddish pink berries. Grouse whortleberry blooms in June and July.

Habitat and Range: Common in open, subalpine forests of the Park, on both sides of the Continental Divide. It also grows in Jdrier forests at lower elevation, but is less common. Its range extends east from British Columbia to Alberta, and south to California, Colorado and South Dakota.

Notes: Grouse whortleberries, like the fruit of other members of the genus *Vaccinium*, are edible. Grouse whortleberry closely resembles low huckleberry (*Vaccinium myrtillus*, previous page), but has hairless twigs and stiffly erect branches. Grouse, mice and chipmunks use them for food. Strong teas made from huckleberries or whortleberries were used by early herbalists as a remedy for typhoid fever. The berry juice has been used as a mouthwash and gargle to heal mouth infections.

Whitestem Gooseberry
Ribes inerme
Gooseberry Family (Grossulariaceae)

Description: Deciduous shrub with erect branches up to 4½ feet tall. Although it is considered a gooseberry, the branches have few (sometimes no) spines. Its leaves are ¾-2½ inches wide and divided into 3 to 5 lobes, like a maple leaf. The lobes are toothed and lobed. The leaves are smooth and hairless, and grow in an alternate pattern along branches. Funnel-shaped flowers (lower photo) are produced in clusters of 2 to 4 from leaf axils. They are greenish to purple-colored and have long, protruding stamens. Its fruit are reddish-purple berries, lacking both hair and glands. They are about ¼ inch in diameter. Whitestem gooseberry blooms in May and June.

Habitat and Range: Whitestem gooseberry is common in the Park's montane forests and shrublands, on rocky slopes and along streams. It occurs in British Columbia and Alberta, and throughout the western United States.

Flower

Notes: Both gooseberries and currants belong to the genus *Ribes*, a word of Arabic origin that means "acid-tasting," in reference to the fruit. The name "gooseberry" refers to the spine-bearing species of *Ribes*, while currants are typically unarmed. The fruit of all gooseberries and currants are edible, but some are more palatable that others. They are full of nutritious compounds, such as Vitamin C, omega 3 and omega 6 fatty acids. Currant and gooseberry fruits have been used by Native Americans to treat uterine and urinary tract problems. Other herbalists have used them to relieve premenstrual symptoms, ease sore throats and fevers, expel worms and as a laxative. They are an important winter food for chipmunks. Always use caution and be sensible with quantity when ingesting wild berries.

Swamp Currant
Ribes lacustre
Gooseberry Family (Grossulariaceae)

Description: Spiny, erect shrub growing 20–40 inches tall. Large, stiff thorns typically occur at branch nodes and bristly spines between nodes, although the thorn pattern along its branches is quite variable. Its leaves are shaped like maple leaves with 3 to 5 palmate lobes. They are shiny above, hairless and ½–3 inches wide. Its flowers are saucer-shaped, brownish pink and hang in drooping clusters, 7 to 15 per group. Each flower is about ½ inch wide. Fruit are black berries sparsely covered with bristly, gland-tipped hairs. They are about ¼ inch wide. Blooms from May to July.

Habitat and Range: Swamp currant is abundant along streams, in the understory of moist to wet forests and in avalanche chutes. It occurs in Alaska, throughout Canada and the western United States. Its range extends eastward from South Dakota into New England, where it occurs from Maine to Virginia.

Notes: Swamp currants are edible and a good source of emergency food. Too many berries, however, may cause stomach cramps and intestinal trouble. Currants have been used in pies, jam and wine. Natives added them to pounded meat to make pemmican. Currants and gooseberries are alternate hosts of white pine blister rust, a fungus that has decimated populations of five-needle pines, such as whitebark pine (pg. 44). A program aimed at ridding the Park of white pine blister rust by eradicating its currants and gooseberries was implemented in the late 1940's and early 1950's. Across the Park crews either dug out plants or sprayed them with herbicide. The program ultimately failed to have any notable effect on white pine blister rust, and the fungus continues to plague whitebark pine populations. See page 14 for more information on the disease caused by white pine blister rust.

Prickly Rose
Rosa acicularis
Rose Family (Rosaceae)

Flower

Description: Deciduous shrub growing 1½–5 feet tall. Its branches are densely to sparsely covered with fine, straight prickles. Wing-like appendages (stipules) are produced at the base of the leaf stalk (petiole). Its leaves are pinnately divided into 5 to 7 leaflets. Each leaflet is elliptic in outline, sparsely hairy and ½–1½ inches long. Solitary flowers are pink and 1–2 inches wide. Fruit are globe- to pear-shaped "rose hips," ¼–¾ inch long. Prickly rose blooms in June and July.

Fruit

Habitat and Range: Prickly rose is common in forests and forest openings in the Park's montane and subalpine zones. Its range extends from Alaska through British Columbia, Idaho and Montana to New Mexico. It occurs across Canada to Nova Scotia. It also occurs throughout much of the northern United States, including most of New England.

Notes: There are 5 different species of rose in Glacier National Park. Prickly rose is most often observed in shady coniferous forests. A similar species, nootka rose (*R. nutkana*, inset photo), grows in open forests in the montane zone. The stems of nootka rose bear fine, straight prickles like prickly rose, but they also have stout, hooked prickles just below the point where the leaf attaches. Nootka rose is mainly a western species; its range extends from Alaska to California and New Mexico. Both nootka rose and prickly rose produce single flowers, which sets them apart from roses with clustered flowers such as Wood's rose (*R. woodsii*, pg. 130) and prairie rose (*R. arkansana*).

Nootka Rose

Baldhip Rose
Rosa gymnocarpa
Rose Family (Rosaceae)

Description: Deciduous shrub with lax stems growing 1–3 feet tall. The stems are sparsely covered with fine prickles. Its leaves are pinnately divided into 5 to 9 leaflets. Each leaflet is elliptic in outline, ¼–1¼ inches long and has gland-tipped teeth along the margin. Its pink flowers are usually solitary and less than 1½ inches across. Fruits are red "rose hips." They are elliptic in outline, less than ½ inch long and lack the small, leaf-like sepals that are present at the tip of the hips produced by our other rose species. Baldhip rose blooms in June.

Habitat and Range: Baldhip rose grows in the understory of montane and lower subalpine forests. It is uncommon in the Park, only occurring west of the Continental Divide. Its range extends from British Columbia south into Washington, Oregon, Idaho, Montana and California.

Notes: In fruit baldhip rose is easy to differentiate from the five other rose species that occur in Glacier National Park because it lacks persistent sepals at the tip of its fruits. Earlier in the season, when roses are blooming, look at the plant's flowers. The petals of baldhip rose are typically smaller (less than an inch long) relative to other roses. The lax growth form of its stems is also diagnostic. Thickets of rose bushes provide important nesting sites and protective cover for grouse and songbirds.

Wood's Rose
Rosa woodsii
Rose Family (Rosaceae)

Description: Deciduous shrub with prickly stems growing 1–5 feet tall. Large, hooked prickles occur in pairs just below the leaf nodes (where leaf meets stem); smaller prickles sparsely to densely cover the branches between nodes. Its leaves are pinnately divided into 5 to 9 toothed leaflets, each ½–1½ inch long and ovate in outline. Teeth along the leaflet margins are often tipped with tiny glands. Flowers are pink to magenta, 5-petaled and 1–2 inches wide. They are produced in clusters of 2 to 5 at branch tips. Fruits are red, berry-like "rose hips" tipped with persistent leaf-like sepals. Blooms in June and July.

Flower

Habitat and Range: Wood's rose is common along the borders of the Park's grasslands, streams and wetlands, and in forest openings. It occurs in Alaska and across Canada from British Columbia to Quebec. In the lower 48 states its range extends from Washington and California east to Wisconsin, Iowa and Texas.

Flruit

Notes: Wood's rose is one of Glacier National Park's most common rose species. It quickly colonizes open ground, especially in moist conditions. Prairie rose (*R. arkansana*) also has clustered pink flowers, but is typically smaller in stature than Wood's rose. Occasionally prairie rose will produce a single flower. Prairie rose is rare in the Park, occurring in grasslands along the Park's eastern boundary. Rose hips can be cooked into stews, made into jam or tea, or eaten raw. They are particularly high in Vitamin C, and are also a good source of Vitamin B, E, K and beta-carotene. Rose petals are also edible.

Subalpine Spiraea
Spiraea densiflora
Rose Family (Rosaceae)

Description: Deciduous shrub with erect branches growing 1½–3 feet tall. Its leaves are ovate in outline and have toothed margins. They are ¾–2½ inches long and have short hairs along the leaf margin. Clusters of tiny, rose-colored flowers are produced in dense, flat-topped clusters at branch tips. In fruit a cluster of 5 capsules forms, each less than ¼ inch long. Subalpine spiraea blooms in July and August.

Habitat and Range: Subalpine spiraea is common in stony soil of the Park's open forest, moist meadows and avalanche slopes in the subalpine zone. It occurs lower but is less common. Its range extends from British Columbia and Alberta south to California, and east to Montana and Wyoming.

Notes: Subalpine spiraea is also known as rose meadowsweet and mountain spiraea. Some botanists call it *Spiraea splendens* var. *splendens*. Rose spiraea (*S. douglasii*) is rare in the Park, collected only once along the edge of a fen near Polebridge. It has pink- to rose-colored flowers borne in a cone-shaped cluster. Various Native American tribes used a tea made from boiled spiraea stem to treat menstrual and abdominal pain and to increase kidney function. White-tailed deer browse the leaves of spiraea in summer and twigs in winter.

SELECTED REFERENCES

Arno, Stephen F. and Ramona P. Hammerly. *Northwest Trees: Identifying and Understanding the Region's Native Trees.* Seattle, WA: The Mountaineers, 1977.

Coombes, Allen J. *Dictionary of Plant Names.* Portland, OR: Timber Press, 1985.

Dorn, Robert D. *Vascular Plants of Montana.* Cheyenne: Mountain West Publishing, 1984.

Kershaw, Linda, Andy MacKinnon and Jim Pojar. *Plants of the Rocky Mountains.* Renton, WA: Lone Pine Publishing, 1998.

Kershaw, Linda. *Edible and Medicinal Plants of the Rockies.* Renton, WA: Lone Pine Publishing, 2000.

Lesica, Peter. *Flora of Glacier National Park.* Corvallis: Oregon State University Press, 2002.

Lesica, Peter. *Manual of Montana Vascular Plants.* Fort Worth, TX: BRIT Press, 2012.

Martin, Alexander C., Herbert S. Zim and Arnold L. Nelson. *American Wildlife and Plants: A Guide to Wildlife Food Habits.* New York: Dover Publications, 1951.

Muenscher, Walter Conrad. *Poisonous Plants of the United States.* New York: Macmillan, 1939.

Phillips, H. Wayne. *Northern Rocky Mountain Wildflowers.* Helena: Falcon Publishing, 2001.

Plowden, C. Chicheley. *A Manual of Plant Names, 2nd ed.* New York: Philosophical Library, 1970.

Rushforth, Keith. *The Easy Tree Guide: Common Native and Cultivated Trees of the United States and Canada.* Guilford, CT: Globe Pequot Press, 2004.

Willard, Terry. *Edible and Medicinal Plants of the Rocky Mountains and Neighbouring Territories.* Alberta: Wild Rose College of Natural Healing, 1992.

GLOSSARY

Achene. A small, dry, seed-like fruit that encloses a single seed.

Alpine. Refers to an altitudinal level where trees are no longer able to successfully establish.

Alternate. A type of arrangement whereby an element such as a leaf occurs singly at each node along a stem or branch.

Armed. Having sharp structures such as spines or thorns.

Ascending. Growing in an upward direction but not strictly erect.

Axil. The upper side of the joint between two structures such as a leaf and stem.

Barb. A short, sharp, backward-facing thorn.

Basal. Positioned at the bottom or base.

Blade. Portion of the leaf that is typically broad and flat, and attached to the stem by the petiole.

Bract. A reduced or modified leaf often closely associated with a flower or flower cluster.

Canopy. The uppermost layer of branches and/or stems. Often used to describe the above-ground structure of a coniferous forest.

Capsule. A dry fruit that splits open at maturity to release seeds.

Catkin. A tight, elongated cluster of unisexual flowers lacking petals and sepals. Usually hanging in a downward, cascading arrangement.

Cone. Reproductive structure of some non-flowering plants that contains seeds or pollen subtended by scale-like bracts. Usually cylindrical.

Corolla. The collective petals of a flower, which may be separate from each other or united into a bowl- or tube-shaped structure.

Crown. The upper portion of a tree's leaves and branches, or the upper portion of plant roots, where they meet the stem.

Deciduous. Dropping or shedding at the end of the growing season. Usually descriptive of leaves.

Dioecious. Plants having only male flowers or female flowers, but not both.

Disturbed. Altered by activities that remove some existing vegetation, such as grazing or plowing.

Drupe. A fruit with a single seed that is enclosed in a stony covering and surrounded by a fleshy exterior (e.g., a cherry or peach).

Elliptic. Oblong or oval in outline, with rounded ends and a wide midsection.

Entire. Smooth along the edge, without teeth or lobes. Often descriptive of leaf margins.

Erect. Strictly upright.

Evergreen. Having foliage that stays green through at least one winter.

Fen. Mineral-rich wetland characterized by organic soil, usually dominated by sedges and mosses.

Fleshy. Referring to tissue that is plump and succulent.

Floodplain. Landform built by deposition of stream gravels through repeated flooding.

Fruit. A mature ovary, complete with any covering tissue that may be present upon ripening.

Genus. A group of plant species that are closely related to each other. A genus may have only one member species.

Gland. A tiny organ that discharges sticky or oily fluid, often appearing like a small colored knob.

Glandular. Gland-bearing.

Glandular-hairy. Bearing hair tipped with tiny glands.

Hybrid. Offspring produced by parents of different species.

Inflorescence. The flower cluster or flower arrangement of a plant.

Introduced. Brought to one continent from another.

Krummholz. A stunted, shrub-like growth form characteristic of trees growing at treeline, caused by windblown snow and exposure to very cold temperatures.

Lateral. On or toward the side.

Leaf axil. The upper side of the joint between a leaf and stem.

Leaflet. Leaf-like subunit of a larger, compound leaf, lacking a bud in its axil.

Lenticel. A lens-shaped dot or pit on bark, through which gaseous exchange may occur.

Linear. Narrow and line-shaped, with essentially two parallel sides.

Lobe. Round or sharp projection that stands out from the margin of a leaf, petal or fruit.

Margin. Outside edge.

Marsh. Wetland characterized by nutrient-rich mineral soil, standing or slow-moving water and non-woody vegetation.

Midrib. Central vein of a structure such as a leaf or bract. Sometimes elevated.

Node. A point along a stem where branches or leaves attach.

Nutlet. A tiny, hard, thick-walled fruit bearing a single seed.

Oblong. Narrowly elliptic but wider toward the tip than the base.

Opposite. Directly across from each other. A description of the placement of leaves along a stem.

Ovary. Female flower structure that contains developing seeds.

Ovate. Oval, but with one end slightly wider than the other. Egg-shaped in outline.

Palmate. Referring to the arrangement of leaflets on a petiole in which all leaflet bases attach to a single point; like the arrangement of fingers on a hand.

Parasitic. Drawing water and/or food from another organism (host) at the host's expense.

Pemmican. A food historically prepared by Native Americans; a mixture of pounded and dried meat and berries.

Perennial. A plant that survives the winter, producing new leaves and flowers each growing season.

Petal. One member of the corolla (the inner, typically colorful and showy series of flower parts).

Petiole. The stalk that attaches a leaf blade to the stem.

Pinnate. Referring to an arrangement of leaflets, lobes or other elements that are positioned opposite each other along a single axis.

Pollen. Tiny, sperm containing particles produced by male reproductive structures (anthers).

Pome. A fleshy fruit with a central, multi-chambered core (e.g., an apple)

Prostrate. Lying on or growing along the ground.

Raceme. A spike-like cluster of stalked flowers that usually begins blooming at the bottom.

Rhizome. An underground stem (often horizontal) with nodes or buds that may sprout above ground.

Riparian. Associated with a river.

Scale. A small, thin, often leaf-shaped structure.

Scree. A collection of rocky, sandy debris. Often occurs on slopes below crumbling rock walls.

Sepal. An individual part of the collective calyx, the outer series of flower parts. Usually green, but may be colorful and showy in some species.

Serotinous. Delayed, as in delayed opening of flowers or cones. Often refers to cones that stay closed for years until high temperatures cause them to open.

Shrub. A plant characterized by woody stems.

Species. A collection of closely related organisms that are capable of inter-breeding and share many discerning characteristics.

Spike. A slender inflorescence with flowers attached directly to an axis.

Stamen. The male portion of a flower, composed of an anther and a filament.

Stipule. An appendage growing at the junction between the leaf and stem.

Style. The long, thin, tubular portion of a female reproductive organ (pistil) between stigma and ovary.

Subtend. To lie just underneath.

Succulent. Refers to tissue that is fleshy, juicy and somewhat thickened.

Talus. A collection of loose, unstable, rocky debris. Typically deposited on a steep slope below a rock wall.

Taproot. The principal descending root produced by some plants.

Terminal. The outermost or uppermost point.

Treeline. The upper elevational limit of successful tree establishment.

Turf. Dense, low-growing vegetation that often forms in moist sites at high elevation. Typically dominated by grasses and grass-like plants.

Vein. A small, tubular structure responsible for transporting water and/ or nutrients. Often visible in the leaf blade of a plant.

Whorl. A collection of 3 or more structures (e.g., leaves or branches) at-tached in a ring around a stem or branch.

Wing. A thin, flat extension protruding from the tip or side of a structure. In the Pea family (Fabaceae), the 2 side flower petals are wings.

Index

Y